GOVERNMENT AND INDUSTRY SERIES
General Editors: J. B. Heath and T. C. Evans

POLITICAL RESPONSIBILITY AND INDUSTRY

POLITICAL
RESPONSIBILITY
AND INDUSTRY

Edmund Dell

London   George Allen & Unwin Ltd
Ruskin House   Museum Street

First published in 1973

© George Allen & Unwin Ltd 1973

ISBN 0 04 322003 7 *hardback*
     0 04 322004 5 *paperback*

Printed in Great Britain
in 11 point Times Roman type
by T. & A. Constable Ltd,
Hopetoun Street, Edinburgh

To Susi

Editors' Preface

That successive governments have mismanaged their relations with British industry seems undeniable. What exactly is wrong, and what are the problems of putting it right, are less easily discerned. Many observers are now asking questions of this kind; they are acutely aware of the importance to this country of finding answers.

The series of books we are now editing examines how governments manage their relations with industry, what the objectives appear to be, how firms manage their responses, and with what effects. There is also a strong prescriptive element running through it. How should government–industry relations be managed, what improvements seem desirable and feasible?

The author of this volume, the Rt Hon. Edmund Dell, MP, is a politician, a former Minister of State at the Board of Trade and at the Department of Employment and Productivity. Thus he has considerable experience of this important area. What he has written is a significant departure from the idea that the government has a simple relationship with industry which could be expressed in economic terms; he is concerned much more with the complex nature of the relationship, the individuals and institutions involved, and the way that people react in their particular circumstances. He has also examined the nature and content of industrial policy in the United Kingdom and some of the problems in its implementation, and he has concluded with practical proposals that are of considerable importance for improving the system of decision and control. Within such a wide subject as industrial policy, he has selected those aspects which seem to him of most significance, and he has used situations with which he had been closely involved as illustrations of his principal themes.

A second volume is being published very shortly. It has been written by Mr Arthur Knight, Deputy Chairman of Courtaulds. While the present volume perceives the problem of government–industry relations through the eyes of a politician and a Minister of the Crown who exercised major responsibilities in relation to British Industry, Arthur Knight has written about the same general subject from the point of view of a senior executive in one of Britain's largest enterprises. The fact that these two leaders in their own fields had sometimes confronted each other in discussion and negotiation, and in their books sometimes touch on the same topics, adds interest and insight into what each has written.

These volumes represent only the personal views of the authors. Each was encouraged to expound his understanding of the general subject in his own way, and neither has a mandate to review or represent any particular range of topics. We felt also that the authors should express themselves in their own individual ways—we had no wish at all to impose uniformity in style or approach.

Of course the views of the authors do not necessarily represent the generality of senior executives or Ministers of the Crown. Nevertheless, as persons who have risen high in their chosen professions, who have had much relevant experience, and who clearly have thought deeply about these experiences, what they have to say is of considerable general interest in understanding more about—and hopefully improving upon —the management of government–industry relations.

The authors of these volumes each had the opportunity to read the manuscript of the other, but only when his own had reached the 'final draft' stage. Each author has added some comments on what the other has written.

There are other volumes in preparation. While these two in the series adopt a 'top-down' approach, two others will adopt rather more of a 'bottom-up' approach in which the same problems will be seen from a quite different standpoint— that of the analyst, both theoretical and practical. Another volume will examine the special problems of local government, and of their relations with the central government and with industry. A final volume will survey all these specialist contributions and will draw more general conclusions.

J. B. HEATH
T. C. EVANS
December 1972

Acknowledgments

There is some pleasure in rounding off a period of one's life by writing down what one thinks one has learnt from it. The period which forms the background of experience on which this book is based began in 1949, when I joined ICI after a spell as a history don at Oxford. It includes the four years during which I held Ministerial office in the Government of Mr Harold Wilson. It may be regarded as ending when, the Industry Act 1972 having reached the statute book and the industrial policies of Mr Heath's Government having turned full circle, I sat down seriously to the task of writing.

I had no intention to provide a programme for the Labour Party. I have however attempted to supply insights into the nature of industrial policy which might perhaps guide a government in their conduct of it.

The book has been read by Anthony Crosland, John Wright, and by the editors of the series. I express my thanks to all of them for their advice.

The publishers provided facilities to make it possible to write the book with the minimum personal effort. I am grateful to the inventor of the dictating machine and to the secretaries at the London Graduate School of Business Studies who typed the various drafts.

Note
The material regarding North Sea Oil on pp. 207-8 was inserted in the text after publication on 1 March 1973 of the First Report of the Public Accounts Committee of Session 1972/3.

EDMUND DELL
14 December 1972

Contents

Part One

DIMENSIONS OF INDUSTRIAL POLICY

Chapter 1

THE IMPORTANCE OF PRAGMATISM

1. *Introduction*

This book is about government relations with industry. In Part One I discuss the responsibilities government is expected to discharge; and in Part Two I discuss the way it discharges them.

The book may be thought therefore to beg the question: does government have such responsibilities? The experience of many centuries of this country's history argues that government does have such responsibilities and that, in some form, it will discharge them.

But this lesson of experience has not escaped challenge, a challenge which I call the 'instinct of *laissez-faire*'. This has been more or less insistent over a long period—certainly extending back to the publication in 1776 of *The Wealth of Nations* by Adam Smith. Its period of maximum impact came in the nineteenth century. But even then it did not really triumph over the inevitable pragmatism of governments, that is their readiness to react in a practical way to practical problems that were presented to them.

It would be surprising if there were not something to be learnt from consideration of an instinct that has been so persistent in our experience. I therefore begin this book by examining the instinct of *laissez-faire*, what it is, and whether it has any value; I shall note also a recent striking demonstration of the compulsions that operate on a government even more than usually imbued with that instinct.

I conclude this chapter by indicating that parallel with the *laissez-faire* instinct there is in this country's past experience an entirely opposed tradition, which I have called the 'imperial tradition'. This also continues to influence current thinking about government relations with industry, but in the precisely opposite direction.

2. *The Instinct of* Laissez-faire

Laissez-faire means government abstention from action on principle, and hence the rejection on principle of responsibility in the social and economic fields.

Certainly the adherents of *laissez-faire* advocated abstention from action in the hope that things would go well, but after the manner of Christian Science they rejected the medicine of intervention even if things went badly. For this reason in fact there has never been a *laissez-faire* government. Some governments however have been motivated by a *laissez-faire* instinct, on occasion very strongly so.

I speak of the instinct of *laissez-faire* because it is far more a feeling about the way government should behave than a principle as to how it should behave. It is a feeling that opposes itself to the strong pressure on government to be pragmatic, to accept the inescapable fact that responsibility will be attributed to it, and to seek ways of discharging that responsibility. This is the dilemma about *laissez-faire*. It cannot realistically imply repudiation of government responsibility for the economy or for industry. Government can disengage from industry. It cannot disengage from responsibility. It can therefore only disengage from industry if it can satisfy its electorate and influential elements in the community that *in practice* there is benefit in it, or at least no harm.

Practical necessity has always ensured that there should be a strong element of pragmatism in the regard that governments and industry would pay to the *laissez-faire* instinct, even at its most influential. Indeed some of this pragmatism was authorised by the founding father, Adam Smith himself, in at least one case—the shipping industry.

This industry has long been among the most important and valuable to Britain. It has also faced some of the toughest state-supported competition, but for that Britain itself provided a precedent. From the middle of the seventeenth century British shipping was supported by the policy of the

Navigation Acts, a policy which required shipment to and from our ports to be made in British bottoms. In general, Adam Smith argued for the international division of labour. 'If a foreign country can supply us with a commodity cheaper than we ourselves can make it, better buy it off them with some part of the produce of our own industry employed in a way in which we have some advantage.'[1] But shipping, in his view, should be an exception to this rule. 'The defence of Great Britain depends very much on the number of its sailors and shipping. The Act of Navigation, therefore, very properly endeavours to give the sailors and shipping of Great Britain the monopoly of the trade of their own country, in some cases by absolute prohibitions and in others by heavy burdens upon the shipping of foreign countries.'[2] Adam Smith attributed this highly discriminatory and protectionist necessity to the requirements of defence. But as the subsequent repeal of the Navigation Acts showed, it was perfectly possible for the Royal Navy to train its own men. Smith was in fact conceding the case for state support where at the time there was strong international competition, that is in shipping, and proposing withdrawal only in those areas of international trade where the Industrial Revolution was in any case winning for Britain a clear competitive lead—an admirably pragmatic point of view. At times, in the same pragmatic interest, exemptions were made in the operation of the Navigation Acts, often despite the opposition of the British shipping industry, where it was found that their effect was to hinder rather than help wider British commercial interests. At times exemptions were made for the benefit of foreign shipping in the hope that other countries would reciprocate, but they did not always do so. In the end, by 1853, the Navigation Acts were repealed.

The British merchant fleet flourished despite repeal because it had become, with the help of this earlier state support and latterly with the help of steam and the substitution of iron for wood in ships, the leading merchant fleet. In other words the ending of state interference in world shipping had become a British interest. If only other states would desist from doing

[1] Adam Smith *Wealth of Nations* (Everyman) vol. I p. 401
[2] ibid. pp. 406-7

what Britain had so successfully done up to that point, the dominance of British shipping would be absolute. William Pitt, after the Battle of Trafalgar, said that Britain had saved itself by its exertions and would as he hoped save Europe by its example. British exertions had raised British shipping to a position which other countries might envy. But the example other countries were likely to follow was the example of the Navigation Acts, not the example of their repeal. It is not surprising that other countries questioned whether Britain, by repealing its two hundred-year-old Navigation Acts at a time when it had become of British interest to do so, had made the withdrawal of state interference in shipping a matter of high international principle.

Today the British shipping industry, together with the Norwegian industry, takes the lead in world shipping in pressing for an end to 'flag discrimination', those practices based on the policy of our Navigation Acts which have been adopted by some other countries, for example in Latin America, to help to develop their own merchant marines. The British shipping industry, understandably, presses the British Government for support in securing an end to flag discrimination. The shipping industry sometimes talks as though it ought to be regarded as that British industry which is today least protectionist, most devoted to *laissez-faire*, not in the Adam Smith version, but in an even more unconditional version. Yet at the same time as it agitates against flag discrimination, the British shipping industry organises itself in shipping conferences and comes to the British Government for investment grants to help with its investment programme. It believes that the British Government has a responsibility to help it compete in the world. The industry is not making enough profit to benefit from free depreciation, which for more profitable industries is a very significant incentive. It wants back the investment grants which were made available to it by the Labour Government. At that time, investment grants for shipping were regarded by our Norwegian competitors as nothing better than state subsidies and quite inconsistent with the principle of free competition in world shipping. At any rate we can be sure that Adam Smith would not have turned in his grave at such a departure from the purest principles of *laissez-faire*.

The history of the shipping industry illustrates the fact that it is sometimes difficult to determine whether a government is acting on principle or pragmatically. It may find some advantage in presenting as the product of principle an action taken on the basis of cold calculation. If a government finds reason to think that certain policies will benefit its economy, that is pragmatism even if those policies are policies of withdrawal from certain areas of economic activity. *Laissez-faire* involves withdrawal even where there is no reasonable expectation, other than that based on faith, that benefit will in fact result. The Corn Laws were repealed in 1846 partly in the expectation that cheaper food would make British manufactures more competitive; and partly in the hope that if Britain withdrew its restrictions on imports of foreign corn, foreign governments would withdraw their restrictions on imports of British manufactures. The first motive might be regarded as pragmatic, the second as principled. There was no reason at all to expect reciprocity, nor was it forthcoming. There is for a government a fundamental difference between doing things which it is convenient to do and which can be changed if its responsibilities require it; and doing similar things for reasons of principle from which it is then more difficult to get unhooked whatever its responsibilities require.

3. *The Educative Experience of Mr Edward Heath*

There are few studies in modern politics more instructive than that of a government evidently attempting to shed some of its responsibilities for reasons apparently of principle. In 1970 a Conservative government came to power under the slogan 'disengagement'. Though no one could really explain what disengagement meant, it was advocated as an important part of an economic policy which was to change the economic fortunes of the nation, by setting free capacities for constructive industrial and commercial activity which had been inhibited by previous policies. The element in the policy that attracted the plaudits of Conservative multitudes was some type of unexplained 'withdrawal' by the State from some types of 'meddling' activity. But what did 'disengagement' mean? It could have meant one of the following things:

   1. *We will do what we can to create an environment in which industry should flourish. We will set free market forces and promote competition. It is then up to industry. If it flourishes, as we expect, well and good. If not, we are not responsible. We will have done all that we should do. To do more would in any case be counter-productive.*

This is something like the supposed position of some nineteenth-century British governments. It was certainly easier to take so unconcerned a line when the political influence of the working class was a great deal less than it is today. But no post-war government, at least until that of Mr Heath, has felt able to shrug its shoulders in advance at economic or industrial calamity. Nor, in the end, could Mr Heath.

Lord Butler described how the first purpose of the Conservative Industrial Charter of 1947 was 'To counter the charge and the fear that we were the party of industrial go-as-you-please and devil-take-the-hindmost, that full employment and the welfare state were not safe in our hands.'[3] The Industrial Charter was to provide proof of concern for ordinary people as well as evidence of an intention to accept 'a responsibility for stimulating industrial efficiency'.[4]

When Mr Heath came to power in June 1970 it was with the professed intention of making a break with such consensus policies. He was setting a ditch not just between himself and his Labour predecessors but between himself and all post-war governments of Britain. He may not have been very explicit about disengagement. Yet there were aspects of this new policy that did seem clear. Symbolic sacrifices of lame ducks were to be part of its educational processes. Death by competition would clear the ground for new and hardy crops of virile industry. Rolls Royce was allowed to go into liquidation. An attempt was made to disengage from shipbuilding on the Upper Clyde. There was to be greater commercial freedom for nationalised industry and a great deal less cosseting of private industry with public money.

3 Lord Butler *The Art of the Possible* (Hamish Hamilton) p. 146
4 ibid.

But it has not worked out that way. This suggests that the second possible interpretation of 'disengagement' is as follows:

2. *We will do what we can to create an environment in which industry should flourish. We have not thought out what we will do if it does not flourish. We hope the question will not arise and meanwhile we will dismantle every policy of our predecessors that was intended to help industry over its difficulties, no doubt in accordance with the same principle that led Julian the Apostate to burn his boats.*[5]

This is certainly more like the policy of disengagement as it was seen in action. The Industrial Reorganisation Corporation was abolished by the Industry Act 1971. Investment grants were withdrawn. Civil servants to whom at the time one spoke sceptically as to how long it would be before the need for instruments of intervention was once more appreciated, replied admiringly that here was a government that knew its mind and would stand by its policies.[6] What they seem not to have noticed was that the policy was based not on principle but on blind hope—or rather on the pretence of principle sustained by blind hope. Hope was disappointed by inflation and growing unemployment, and the policy of disengagement was rapidly abandoned, its only victim Palmers Hebburn ship-repairing yard on the Tyne. Thereafter came rapidly, one after the other, the rescue of the Mersey Docks (at great expense to the bondholders but at greater expense to the government), the nationalisation of Rolls Royce, capital injections for Cammell Laird, a vast outpouring of public money on the Upper Clyde and, most symbolic of all to a Socialist, £70 million of naval orders brought forward, not because the ships were needed for defence but because military work was needed to create employment.

By March 1972 there came the announcement of the restoration of investment grants in development areas and of

[5] This incident was immediately followed by the death of Julian in battle and the defeat of his army. The reference in the text therefore seems more appropriate than one to Hernan Cortes whose burning (or sinking) of his boats led on to the conquest of Mexico.

[6] It is fair to say that civil servants are afraid of being accused, by an incoming government, of attempting to frustrate their policies.

the creation within the Department of Trade and Industry of the Industrial Development Executive, an agency superficially reminiscent of the IRC. The Industry Act 1972 was introduced to authorise these measures. Having burnt one set of boats, they built another by the light of the dying fire. For all these steps, for all these departures from declared policy, individual justifications could be provided. But taken together they were so clearly at odds with the original intention that disengagement did not merely die, it died laughing. The nationalised industries had not even had a breathing space from government interference. The battle against inflation had led to their use as a battering ram against the wage claims of their employees. Once more the country found itself with an interventionist government equipped with the usual set of crude instruments. What had defeated the government was the fact of responsibility. There was a crisis of inflation and unemployment and the government had the responsibility for dealing with it. It could not be deflected from the use of any weapon of policy that seemed relevant, however instinct moved it. Pragmatism had to take precedence over principle, and over instinct too.

Since these events there has been some attempt to suggest a third meaning for 'disengagement':

3. *Of course all governments have to intervene in industry. We will just try to do it less than did our predecessors and leave more to market forces.*[7]

In other words, it was all a matter of degree. But if it is a matter of degree and not of principle, then the degree will be determined not by policy but by the pressures. If there is more pressure there will be more, not less, intervention. So in fact it has turned out. Instead of disengagement, we have the most lavish intervention in history.

This then is the logical dilemma at the core of *laissez-faire* and of all policies inspired by it. What does a government *do* if *laissez-faire* does not work? The answer is, it intervenes. So

7 See for example Ronald Butt in *The Times*, 28 September 1972: 'it remains true that, subject to providing for special circumstances, and people who need to be taken care of, the government sticks to its policy of letting those who can stand on their own feet. But this simply is not understood.'

it has been throughout the history of *laissez-faire* and derivatives such as disengagement. Governments cannot rest from responsibility. They can only seek new and more hopeful ways of discharging their responsibility. That is why it is right to describe *laissez-faire* as an instinct. It is an instinct about the way government should discharge its responsibilities—if it can.

4. Laissez-faire *as Criticism*

The question thrown up by the educative experience of Mr Heath is this: Why, in this country particularly, have we been confronted by repeated epidemics of these unexplained withdrawal symptoms, by this kind of governmental autism— despite overwhelming and continuing evidence that the State is and must be deeply involved in the economic life of the nation?

It would be wrong to imagine that questions of this kind have the simple answers that Keynes found persuasive, or at least attractive. The 'madmen in authority who hear voices in the air' may not as he thought have simply been 'distilling their frenzy from some academic scribbler of a few years back'.[8] There have always been available a variety of academic scribblers from whom a variety of different frenzies— protectionist as well as *laissez-faire*—could have been distilled. It is the choice of scribbler that is significant and it is the *laissez-faire* instinct that has dictated the choice. The theorists of *laissez-faire* have now, most of them, passed into history. J. B. Conant tells of a Harvard Professor of the 1870s, since forgotten, who used to tell his class 'the reason that everyone now believes in the wave theory of light is that all those who once believed in the corpuscular theory are dead'[9] —a story which shows that even in the physical sciences one can be both dead and right. Death has not sufficed to kill *laissez-faire*. The instinct survives, and it is this survival after death for which one would wish an explanation.

No doubt the answer is to be found in part in the historical

8 J. M. Keynes *The General Theory of Employment, Interest and Money* (Macmillan) p. 383
9 J. B. Conant *Science and Common Sense* (OUP) p. 29

experience of this country, an experience substantially different for example from that of France or Germany; in the relationship of the commercial and industrial classes to royal and then aristocratic government, in the relationship of non-conformity to a state church, and in the fact of industrial leadership at a time when *laissez-faire* influences were at their strongest—when indeed they could be at their strongest because of the fact of British industrial leadership. But something must be allowed for the element of pertinent criticism of the way we manage our affairs to which the *laissez-faire* instinct gives voice.

In fact the practical effect of the surviving residue of *laissez-faire* is by no means entirely unhealthy. It compounds suspicion with scepticism and brings both together in the conviction that these days too many things are done which cannot be justified by clear criteria or by much prospect of achieving the supposed objective. Most worrying of all is so-called 'selective intervention'.

The scepticism leads to questioning as to whether the proposed remedies really provide a solution to the indicated problem. One problem is the slow rate of economic growth. The slow rate of growth is one reason why governments do not merely hold the ring and use general pressures, such as the pressure of demand, but fussily intervene. Yet there is little evidence that these interventions in fact do much for the rate of economic growth, at any rate in the short term, and there is a great deal of evidence of the dangers.

Government can make big errors. Because of its command over national resources it can by its errors distort a whole sector of activity, in the way that engineering in this country has been distorted by our commitments to aerospace and nuclear energy. It can create vested interests which will not have to live by any commercial test of viability, which will employ highly articulate people who will lobby most effectively against any possibility of redundancy when their usefulness in their present jobs has gone. 'Do not dissolve our research team' they will say. 'Do not cast our labour on the market or we will emigrate and you will lose a great national resource to the Americans.'

Scepticism can be some safeguard. The suspicio
the motives both of businessmen and of governme...
nessmen are thought of as protectionist by nature and intent
on conspiracy against competition. As for government, it is
feared that its actions when it becomes deeply involved in
the affairs of industry and commerce, when it departs from
simply holding the ring and perhaps providing general
incentives, will be a mere response to pressure and probably
wasteful of the nation's resources. At best, though most
expensive, the efforts of government may be devoted to some
prestige project which may elevate the national pride while
reducing the national income. At worst, though usually
cheaper, electoral calculation may determine action, a lame
duck may be rescued, and the nation be, in effect, asked to
buy votes on behalf of the government party. Governmental
policies *should* be continually tested against their stated
objectives. In so far as it helps to ensure that this is done, the
laissez-faire instinct is a not unwelcome component of our
national tradition.

5. Laissez-faire *in Retreat*
If one examines what it was, historically, that even in Britain
pushed back the frontiers of *laissez-faire*, four main influences
can be identified. One was international competition, which
eventually compelled the re-erection of protective tariffs.
Britain never won from other countries the reciprocity that
its free trade policies were intended to inspire. But when after
World War II it became possible to achieve reciprocity by
negotiation, Britain devoted itself to it with an enthusiasm
born of priority in example. It was as though Britain had a
peculiar property in free trade due to its nineteenth-century
pioneering. There was an almost audible sigh of relief at this
reversion to freer trade after the relapse represented by tariff
reform.

The second influence was the emergence, largely under the
impact of industrial development, of specific social requirements that could not be met without the intervention of the
State. The government machine has had to be built up to
meet these requirements. The success of British industry and

commerce without government help seemed at first to imply that there was no need for big government. On the contrary, the resources of government were kept small as a matter of policy, and that fact limited what the government could do even if it was called upon. Small government meant inexpert government. Only gradually was the need for expertise in government appreciated. The philosophical mind of the British aristocrat, pondering the future of the British Empire, did not need to be tinged with any awareness of matters relating to the terms of trade or commercial treaties. When a British government wished to negotiate a trade treaty with France in 1860 they asked Cobden to do it for them. Even the British Army did not have to be efficient. It was more important to have an active and efficient civil service in India than in Britain, because there the role of government was more obviously crucial. Only gradually was it realised that a civil service based on a principle of selectivity other than patronage might be desirable in Britain too if services increasingly seen to be essential were to be provided. Appropriately enough, the sewage demands of an industrial society created a first, imperative, requirement for action by government and therefore for expertise in government. Then came education, then the deployment of labour with Beveridge's Labour Exchanges. In sewage, education and the deployment of labour, the requirements were both urgent and specific. They could therefore be met with specific answers in the form of drainage systems, schools and labour exchanges.

It is easier for government to act and to acquire the necessary expertise for action where requirements are specific. In the early years after the war, the National Health Service was created to meet one such specific requirement. Today when there is an increasing demand for greater protection of the environment against pollution of all kinds, specific complaint can again lead to specific remedy, although no one should imagine that even in these areas solutions which are efficient in the use of resources are readily found.

This takes us to the third factor, which has been an increasing recognition of the divergences that so frequently arise between private and social costs. These divergences have become increasingly obvious in the every-day awareness of pollution, congestion and redundancy; and are illustrated also by the ever more important activities of multinational companies which, in looking after themselves, can in certain circumstances damage their hosts. Governments have been concerned to find ways by which they can ensure that costs caused to society by private activities are charged to those who give rise to them.

The fourth factor in the story has been a developing sense, as the twentieth century wears on, of economic failure. Since the war there has been an increasing consciousness of the fact that our economic growth rate has been slow relative to that of our principal industrial competitors. But the greatest single impact was made by unemployment between the wars, by the world economic crisis of the 1930s and, indeed, by belief in the success the Soviet Union had achieved in speeding growth and eliminating unemployment by means of planning. The idea of planning—the belief that the human intellect can command and control the social and economic environment—has long been part of Socialist thinking. After the war, with the mounting anxiety about our economic performance, the idea, in a more modest form, penetrated Conservative thinking too. By 1962 Selwyn Lloyd, as Chancellor of the Exchequer, had established the National Economic Development Council. Post-war governments in fact developed a large battery of devices for promoting economic growth: investment incentives, industrial training boards, economic development committees, export services, advisory services of various kinds, pre-production contracts. Governments of both political parties competed in ingenuity in the creation of such devices. Political and economic necessity became the mother of interventionist invention. The highest point of inventiveness was reached during the Government of Harold Wilson with the creation of a Ministry of Technology and of the Industrial Reorganisation Corporation. Then, at the very moment at which the Wilson Government was reaching this apogee of inventiveness, Conservatives began thinking of dismantling even what they themselves had created during their thirteen years of continuous responsibility. After all, had not the results of all their devices been rather disappointing? The Wilson devices represented even greater interference with those market forces to which the Conservative Party was now turning for salvation. The ideological battle opened up again, not about socialism but about how far the future of the capitalist elements in a mixed economy could be left to the mercy of market forces. It opened up because disillusioned Tories were turning back towards *laissez-faire*, not because the Wilson Government was making dramatic new strides towards Socialism. The political battle had moved right: for Labour, intervention rather than public ownership; for the Tories, market forces rather than the Industrial Charter.

So the search for a straight and simple route to economic salvation turned the Tories back towards *laissez-faire*. It was not *laissez-faire* that in reality they proposed. There would be no question of the Government renouncing responsibility if these policies failed. In any case the changes they were proposing were at the periphery of economic policy. Only the most desperate and, at the same time, optimistic interpretation of the consequences of disengagement could have led anyone to suppose that such changes could provide much by way of positive prospects for the British economy. Now with the Industry Act 1972, and the massive powers of intervention contained in it, all idea of disengagement has gone. Government has been dragged back to face the fact that in order to discharge its responsibilities it must have a capacity to intervene, that it cannot exclude itself on principle from the possibility of action. Yet the feeling remains that it is withdrawal that is right and that intervention is only politically convenient.

This then is what the *laissez-faire* instinct is today. First it is a hankering after a truth that has been abandoned for political reasons; a solution that has been rejected because for a democracy the road is too hard. Secondly, it is a criticism of easy, ill-considered, insufficiently justified, and sometimes profligate interventions. The criticism could be met if it were possible to develop clear criteria and to show specific needs and specific remedies. About the hankering, nothing can be done. In British political mythology the State is in some sense sinful. So it will remain, at least until we find some way of pouring over it the holy waters of success.

6. *The Imperial Tradition*

The *laissez-faire* instinct in British government is paralleled by the imperial tradition. I have shown how the *laissez-faire* instinct expresses deep feelings that governments do more than they can justify, and accept responsibilities that they should not even try to discharge. The imperial tradition has expressed the continuing responsibility of governments to act positively for the good of their own people even at the expense of the interests of foreigners.

The imperial tradition has been built of war, conquest, discrimination in trade, the Navigation Acts, the use of power when Britain had power to use. Joseph Chamberlain argued to the British working classes that their interest was in the preservation of empire. The trade which gave them employment depended upon it. Reciprocal obligation within a preferential imperial system was the key to Britain's future prosperity. One cannot grant preferences unless one has tariffs. Therefore there must be 'tariff reform', a euphemism for the erection of a tariff system within which there could be imperial preference. In the Joseph Chamberlain conception, international trade was a more civilised form of war. Alliances, such as the Commonwealth and Empire, had to be forged to conduct the war successfully. International trade was, as Clausewitz might have put it, the prosecution of power politics by other means.

Throughout history, governments have thought it normal to promote national trade through the use of state power. No government did this more extensively, more persistently, or more successfully than did the British government before the nineteenth century. Then, with success, with industrial leadership, came *laissez-faire*, a civilising force to the extent that it mitigated the use of power. With the growth of competition from Germany and the United States of America at the end of the nineteenth century, came Joseph Chamberlain and tariff reform. Competition had forced a relapse from liberal attitudes. Still later, the loss of empire as an instrument of demand management left Britain uncertain and divided between the *laissez-faire* instinct and the use of state power.

But the imperial tradition was not worked out. If we were not to enjoy the prestige of empire, we would seek prestige through advanced technology, by becoming leaders in aerospace and nuclear energy. Only with lavish state aid could it be done. Military requirements encouraged its doing. It was expensive but it was consistent with our honourable desire for world leadership in some fields at least.

Doubtful as governments might be of their ability to promote economic development in general, in aerospace and nuclear energy they seemed to have no doubt. Though the costs far exceeded the costs of empire, they have gone on. They have spent magnificently. They have done everything that in other fields they had refused to do. They have demonstrated national political will. They have dragooned British customers. They have compulsorily rationalised British industries. There has been no question here of *voluntary* rationalisation such as was undertaken by the IRC. They have set up permanent government agencies, the Atomic Energy Authority, the Ministry of Aviation in its various incarnations, and enormous research laboratories. They have gone further in intervention than even the Japanese government is believed to do. They have reconciled themselves to the frequent cancellation of great projects undertaken at vast but unforeseeable expense and to the waste that has inevitably ensued. They have created not just aircraft and nuclear power plants but deeply entrenched vested interests that demand more and ever more by way of resources if they are to be satisfied. They have done everything but enjoy themselves. The costs have been too high for that, and all the time the nagging feeling that governments should not do this sort of thing has eaten away at any possibility of a relaxed contemplation of technological white elephants. Not for them the carefree attitude which the French have brought to their commitment to Concorde. Here, instead of commitment, there has been questioning. But the pressures of national prestige and of the thousands of persons employed in these industries are likely to determine the nation's future course rather than any more scientific calculations regarding investment and return.

But, as part of the spin-off from the national effort in aerospace and nuclear energy, the belief grew that perhaps something of what has been done for the advanced technologies could be done for industry generally. So in 1964 Harold Wilson was elected to office as leader of a white-hot technological revolution which would use the resources of aerospace to fertilise industry generally. The fertilisation would take place by joining the Ministry of Aviation to a new Ministry of Technology. Osmosis would do the rest.

The problem one has not yet solved is always the most difficult. One may promote trade by the creation of empire. One may create advanced technology industries by the expenditure of vast sums of money. But how does a government diffuse into industry generally managerial skill, entrepreneurial insight, energy in marketing, quality in production? The imperial tradition preserves the problem without providing the answer.

Chapter 2

THE CONCEPT OF INDUSTRIAL POLICY

'Whoever sets himself to base his political thinking on a re-examination of the working of human nature, must begin by trying to overcome his own tendency to exaggerate the intellectuality of mankind.

'We are apt to assume that every human action is the result of an intellectual process by which a man first thinks of some end which he desires, and then calculates the means by which that end can be obtained.'

Graham Wallas *Human Nature in Politics*

1. *Industrial Policy as a Protective Device*

Laissez-faire is, and has always been found to be, inconsistent with the political responsibilities of government. Industrial policy is a collection of varied responses to the different kinds of political responsibility imposed on government by the changing requirements and circumstances of industry. The objectives include support for domestic industry and encouragement to the location of mobile investment in one's own territory rather than that of foreigners. These varied responses have always had at least one thing in common. They were born out of some concept of British interests. They were intended to promote British interests or the interests of some part of the British community. The interests of foreigners were entirely secondary and were considered only to the extent that it was necessary to do so to promote British interests.

More recently doubt has sometimes been expressed, particularly by businessmen, as to whether British governments have not forgotten the priority they must give to British interests. These doubts arise from the post-war development of international collaboration in economic affairs and from the special facilities now given to imports from less developed countries. Undoubtedly these developments have involved compromises in which the interests of particular British industries have not been safeguarded as they would wish. They have also had their effect on the type of instrument of industrial policy available to government. There is nothing new in one interest being sacrificed for the sake of another which seemed more important; or indeed of one British industry being sacrificed for the sake of another. In the nineteenth century British agriculture was sacrificed for the supposed benefit of British manufacture. The fact that British governments have sought to discharge their responsibilities in part by promoting international trade, does not mean any abandonment of priority for British interests—though no doubt bad and inconsistent decisions can be made in pursuit of any policy. The responsibility of government, when an industry contracts under the impact of international competition, is to ensure the availability of alternative employment.

The fundamentally protective nature of industrial policy is illustrated by the instruments it uses and has used. In the past the principal weapon of industrial policy was military conquest of markets for one's industries. This is no longer practicable or acceptable outside the Communist bloc. Some developed countries of the West may still have their spheres of influence amongst less developed nations, but few of these are major markets for industrial goods, the most important being the other developed countries themselves.

The tariff, the quota and the non-tariff barrier are more civilised instruments of protective industrial policy. The continuing importance of the tariff should not be underrated. Its significance is partly blurred by the use of averages which conceal the very high tariffs that still protect many important industrial commodities in all the developed countries. Quotas continue to operate particularly on some imports from Communist bloc countries and less developed countries. The non-tariff barrier is everything other than the tariff that impedes the free operation of international competition. Thus the Navigation Acts constituted a non-tariff barrier. Differences in statutory national standards, for example of safety in operation, can be a very powerful form of non-tariff barrier. The most powerful of all is probably the

B

nationalistic purchasing policy of governments and state enterprises which buy virtually exclusively from national suppliers and continue to do so even in free trade areas and common markets.

Since the war, nations have decided that objectives concerned with both peace and prosperity will be served by a rapid increase in international trade, and to that end tariffs and quotas have been, in considerable part, negotiated away. The non-tariff barrier is more difficult to eradicate. The success of any negotiations to dismantle non-tariff barriers would depend on a high degree of trust between nations because it can be very difficult to prove the motivation of a buyer's behaviour. For example if it continued to be the case that 100 per cent of Japanese shipping was built in Japan, it might be very difficult to be satisfied that this was purely because of such superior competitiveness in all departments of Japanese shipbuilding that not even one or two ships could be allowed to escape. But Japanese shipbuilding *is* very competitive. It is often very difficult to prove that governments and state enterprises have not good commercial reasons for their purchasing policies. Yet the availability of a base load of orders from national utilities is obviously of importance to their national suppliers. It is of particular importance to British industry, and this non-tariff barrier is likely to be the subject of continuing debate within EEC, continuing both because of the protective instincts of governments and because of their uncertainty as to the industrial consequences of letting it go.

Since the war, industrial policy in this country has been dominated conceptually as well as financially by the advanced technologies. This is another example of the protective nature of industrial policy, although in its working out it has, in this case, sometimes been found necessary to seek protection on a European rather than on a purely national basis. At the end of the war we had large numbers of scientists and engineers skilled in nuclear physics and in the design and construction of aircraft and aero-engines, as well as some mathematicians and scientists who were opening new paths in computer technology. For a combination of military and political reasons a considerable proportion of the resources devoted in this country to technology was invested in these people. Indeed, it seemed obvious that these people constituted a valuable national resource whose use would promote great economic benefit. The problems were, however, very different from any met before in other technological industries such as the chemical industry. The time-scale was long, the technological risks very great, the research and development costs very high. The need for economy could frustrate the search for the best options.

The USA constituted a very large proportion of the world market but had its own rapidly developing advanced technology industries, supported by defence and space expenditure. The USA could provide its own industries both with an enormous domestic market and with a base for export sales. Such competition greatly reduced the export prospects of the British industries whose domestic market was ever more insufficient as a support for ever more expensive research and development. The world market was thus strongly biased against a fruitful exploitation of British skill in the advanced technologies.

If Britain's position in the field was to be held at all, public money would be not just an aid or an incentive. It would be the condition of bare survival. For a country with scarce resources and slow economic growth, only history, national pride and political pressure could justify such expenditures in competition with the American giant. But technology seemed to have become an end in itself, an expression of national purpose, not needing economic justification. When economic considerations were raised, there was talk of 'spin-off' which would compensate indirectly for the direct and expensive failures. The idea of a 'Ministry of Technology' caught the popular belief that technology was a thing in itself in which the nation could have a special pride, and that in spin-off some industrial justification for the expenditure would at last be found.

In conception, the Ministry of Technology was the high point of the technological illusion. In practice, under the compulsion of economic constraints, the Ministry began the difficult and exhausting battle back towards industrial reality. It was found that whenever industrial policy was dominated by technology rather than by the market, it went wrong. Soon the Ministry of Technology was calling itself a Ministry of Industry. Technology was a means, but the end was the market which industry was to supply. In the advanced technologies, the market was under political constraints and was little subject to the ordinary rules of international competition. Therefore the way to secure a market was through international collaborative agreements. The way to a nation's market was through the heart of that nation's government. If a government saw the prospect of employment for its people in these prestigious fields, it would provide the market for the eventual product. Particularly was this true in aerospace. International collaborative agreements were also a way of reducing each nation's share of the development costs, though perhaps at the price of the total being increased due to the frictions of international agreements. The existence of such agreements does not mean that European nations have abandoned their own dreams of national technological splendour. The dominance of the USA remains as an incitement to high endeavours. Even Britain, which has learnt the hardest lessons and experienced the harshest economic pressures, cannot reconcile itself entirely to the thought that advanced technology, like dyestuffs technology, is just a matter of industrial economics.

Industrial policy thus finds sustenance in that characteristic of nation states which leads them to refuse to submit to the logic of economic calculation: pride, and the desire to be in the race, though the prize be to the swiftest. After all there are many gold medals to be distributed in these games. If we can find a way of concentrating our efforts, we may still win some. There is, for example, the fast breeder reactor, still our claim to leadership in nuclear energy.

It was not the advanced technology industries alone that some nations segregated from normal international competition. Agriculture has always been a special case, for social and political reasons, and indeed, though it was sacrificed by

Britain in the nineteenth century, it was understood to be a special case even by Adam Smith and is now once more regarded as a special case in Britain. It has always been accepted that nations will wish to retain, if they can, a national source of military supplies. Shipbuilding is another industry which many countries placed in the specially protected class at a time when Britain was still putting it in the competitive class.

Thus industrial policy is to be seen as an expression of nationalism, or sometimes now Europeanism, in international affairs. When these days industrial policy is spoken of in a European context it expresses an intention—backed when necessary by public money—to have certain specific industries in Europe whatever the international competitive situation may be at the moment. A European industrial policy is likely to be concerned with projects in the advanced technology industries which the separate national governments find too expensive to sustain singly; with the protection of certain industries such as shipbuilding which are under strong competitive attack and which may be more securely protected on a continental rather than on a national basis; and with the creation, again as a response to the competitive strength of the great American 'multinational' companies, of European companies—which may be facilitated by the formulation of a European company law. European industrial policy is almost exclusively an expression of the politics of Europeanism rather than of economic or social need, though this might change if a European regional policy was developed. National industrial policies have a similar political aspect, but not so exclusively.

There is a social dimension to industrial policy, and here again it is often protective in character. The most contro-versial occasions on which this social dimension emerges is in the rescue of lame ducks. Indeed these are the occasions when industrial policy achieves star billing. Confusion is caused by the fact that it is always considered necessary on such occasions, in face often of the deepest public scepticism, to proclaim that in due course the cripple will walk normally again on his own two feet. It is evidently that prospect alone that makes so socially minded an intervention respectable. Wages may not be paid unless there is the prospect of a return to viability. Nor for that matter will pride permit them to be accepted except on that condition. Therefore what is in fact an intervention for social purposes, to provide an opportunity for men to find alternative work, to give the government time to find new industry for the area, is usually described as an intervention for economic purposes, to restore a defunct company to health. Confusion is added by the fact that sometimes it really is possible to do just that. So it is always a little uncertain what the government really has in mind. At this moment, is government assistance to shipbuilding motivated by the belief that the industry can be made competitive or by the need to support employment? In a recent Treasury Minute to the Public Accounts Committee it says: 'it may . . . be necessary to take wider regional and employment considerations into account when considering any further assistance to the industry.'[1] If the objective of policy is to protect employment in a particular industry, then that consideration will take priority over any consideration of the competitiveness of that industry in an international context.

The social dimension of industrial policy is one of the few aspects from which governments can expect to gain short-term political dividends. For the most part the political impact of industrial policy is blunted by the fact that almost everything constructive that it can achieve accrues only in the long term. Rescue operations and large government-supported export deals alone may have the immediate politically beneficial effect of saving employment in the short term. But the rest, whether it be training, selective assistance to particular industries, restructuring, or promoting competition, will yield its dividend well beyond the next election. This was true even with the Labour Government's Aluminium Smelter Project. The successful conclusion of the negotiations in 1968 held out a promise to excitable nationalist opinion. But the first

[1] Treasury Minute on the Reports from the Committee of Public Accounts (Cmnd S 126) p. 7

smelter was actually opened in Anglesey in 1971 by the Conservative Secretary of State for Wales.

When we move away from those industries which, for various reasons, nations desire to segregate from international competition, we find that industrial policy, though it is still protective in the sense that it acts to strengthen national industry or influence the location of mobile international industry, does not necessarily inhibit international trade. The steps taken since the war, through the General Agreement on Tariffs and Trade and otherwise, to remove barriers to international trade, have had their influence on the types of instrument used by industrial policy. Whereas the older instruments are directly protectionist against international competition, the newer instruments are intended to work in an ambience of growing international competition.

Trade barriers are being replaced by subsidies or incentives —to invest, to export, to train, to move industry into development areas and to move workers out of development areas. It is sometimes claimed that these incentives or subsidies are not so very different from trade barriers. They are supposed to be non-discriminatory. Investment incentives, for example, are available to assist the purchase of foreign machinery at the same rates at which they assist the purchase of British machinery. But they are certainly discriminatory in their intention to strengthen British industry and therefore its competitiveness internationally, as well as in the objective of influencing the location of mobile investment by attracting it to Britain. They can also be discriminatory between domestic industry and foreign investment. For example, there are forms of assistance made available to ICL, the British computer firm, which are not likely to be available also to IBM. Yet whether or not there is a difference in principle between incentives and barriers, there has certainly been a difference in effect. The barriers held back the flow of international trade. The incentives have not proved inconsistent with a dramatic rise in international trade. They do not seem to have had an adverse effect on international trade, possibly the contrary. This does not mean that there are not still types of government intervention which are autarchic in their effect, and one famous example of this—the aluminium smelter project—is described later.

The OECD Committee presided over by Jean Rey, which reported in 1972, said this:

> To the extent that certain aspects of industrial policy are intended to increase efficiency, reduce costs, develop skills, improve technical education and promote a more competitive environment, they help to maintain and increase the genuine comparative advantage of a country's industry and therefore cannot be considered objectionable as regards their effect on international trade.[2]

The categories of expenditure which the Committee regarded as unobjectionable comprise expenditure on basic research, training, education and public investment in industrial infrastructure. They added that some industrial policy measures 'however respectable their objectives may be, nevertheless distort trade and interfere with the optimal international division of labour'.[3] They are therefore to be classified as non-tariff barriers.

If the only unobjectionable categories of expenditure are those listed by the Rey Committee, this country certainly operates, through its industrial policy, a wide range of non-tariff barriers. But, oddly enough, UK industrial policy has developed hand in hand with an explosion in its international trade. The Rey Committee does concede: 'Government cannot, solely in the interests of international trade, follow a policy of complete nonintervention in the activities of industry'.[4] Despite this bow in the direction of the facts of democratic life, the Committee's comments on industrial policy illustrate a tendency to write down the essential role of national governments, in the supposed interest of maximising international trade.

But however much governments may themselves some-

---

[2] OECD *Policy Perspectives for International Trade and Economic Relations* para. 143
[3] ibid. para. 144
[4] ibid. para. 145

times wish not to intervene, the national state does exist and does have responsibilities. It exists, therefore it intervenes. It is an odd economic conception that of all the forces that may operate in a market, governments alone must be prohibited from taking direct action to strengthen their nation's economic and industrial structure, however powerful their conviction that they can act usefully in that sense. It is true that government action has been used to support aggressive competitive raids on the economies and industries of other countries. That is a use of industrial policy that can rightly be held objectionable. A prime motive of government action has been the provision of incentives to raise employment and to create competitive industries. This is certainly a type of competition which it is sensible to control. But provided these uses of industrial policy are controlled, there is no reason why, if they believe they know ways of doing so, governments should not contribute to the process of national enrichment. One key question is whether government intervention is employed for the purpose of running large and persistent balance of payments surpluses. If it is not, then any increase in exports is balanced by an increase in imports and the nation's enhanced prosperity is contributed to by foreign as well as domestic suppliers.

There is of course the theoretical danger that international trade could become an exchange of heavily subsidised products with no real increase in international welfare resulting from it. This is unlikely. Outside the few industries which are sustained on public money for largely non-economic reasons, industrial policy in this country does not deploy resources large enough to have such an effect. Leaving aside the two major areas of aerospace and nuclear energy, all the selective interventions of the Ministry of Technology added together were very cheap by the standards of government expenditure. They showed that a large number of sensible and helpful things could be done at low cost. Their low cost does suggest that their total economic effect would be small. Nevertheless cost is not always a proper measure of value to the economy. Thus DTI's export services are provided at low cost, but are of considerable importance to industry in general. Since the war there has been a gradual increase in moderate, restrained, inexpensive, almost unnoticed, support from the State for British industry. It is frequently forgotten how much was achieved, with how little publicity and controversy, and with how few failures, through assistance under the Local Employment Acts (now repealed but substituted by similar powers under the Industry Act 1972).

The cause of international trade would be better served if the role of nation states was recognised not ignored. It might then be possible to negotiate rules of international trade which would provide nation states with an incentive to reduce, not increase, their autarchic arrangements and their nontariff barriers. This would require a treaty or convention. Not a treaty of the kind that is negotiated at the end of a war, but one which regulates by what rules war may be carried on—the Geneva Convention rather than the Treaty of Versailles! The object is not to eliminate competitive intervention in international trade but to civilise it; to reduce the extent to which gains are made at the expense of other nations rather than in co-operation with other nations; and to make the rules of competition not too violently opposed to the rules and pressures that govern the activities of national governments. The nation state is inevitably a protective device. It has the responsibility of defending the standard of life of its people. International co-operation is one method of discharging that responsibility. There is therefore no reason why international co-operation should not be developed provided that the nature of the nation state is understood. A treaty which made it easier for nations at full employment to achieve equilibrium in their balance of payments would in itself be an incentive to them to reject autarchy, to lower non-tariff barriers, and to concentrate their action on policies leading to more competitive and efficient industries, rather than to support for industries than can only exist because they are protected and subsidised. Such incentives to governments to see their interests in moving in that direction are an essential supplement, above all where non-tariff barriers are concerned, to whatever can be achieved by international regulation in reducing obstacles to the development of international trade.

2. A Calculated Use of Market Forces

We have an economic system which is actually working. Its working is in many respects defective. The political parties differ about the extent and nature of the defects. Politics is in large part concerned with controversy about the identification and correction of these defects. There are many aspects of the system which are not understood: why for example in different countries it releases human potential to such different extents; why one country can expand its production so much faster than another and why, indeed, in some countries there has been so little expansion at all. There is no sign of policies becoming available which would increase the UK rate of economic growth to that of Japan. Indeed the connection between policy and the rate of economic growth is only dimly apprehended, at best. Yet as Galileo might have said, *e pur si muove*. The system does move. There is a complex of relationships between people as producers and consumers, a complex which changes over time, but which has, in the developed countries at least, enabled people to benefit from technological innovation and to improve their standards of life. What can industrial policy add?

Industrial policy is frequently presented as part of a policy for promoting economic growth; but for much of industrial policy, this is an inappropriate context. Industrial policy is in part concerned with improving the efficiency with which the nation's resources are used. Thus, for example, it is concerned with competition policy—an aspect of industrial policy which is so important as to deserve a separate chapter. It is also concerned with general incentives, such as incentives to investment, which it is hoped will increase the economy's capacity to expand, a hope based on the observation that in some other countries whose economies are growing much faster than our own, there is a much higher rate of investment. If competition policy and general incentives of this kind achieve their purpose they may have some effect on the rate of growth, though it is an effect that is likely to be imperceptible in the short run.

But much of industrial policy is concerned with so-called

'selective interventions'. These range from the fabulously expensive, as in the case of Concorde, to research and development contracts let at a cost of some thousands of pounds. They vary greatly in their importance to the industries affected by them. For many industries they are of only marginal significance. These interventions have to be justified on an individual basis, by their effect perhaps on a group of assets gathered in one particular firm, rather than by any supposed macro-economic effect on the rate of growth of the economy as a whole. Some of these interventions are politically or socially motivated and, while being by some judgments of the public interest perfectly justifiable, may have a negative effect on the rate of economic growth. Thus, for example, the diversion of resources to aerospace may have such an effect. Rescue operations can have the effect of slowing the adaptation of an industry to a changing competitive situation.

These calculations are very difficult to make. It is an illusion to imagine that because direct economic effects sometimes seem more calculable, governments can ignore political or social effects. Indeed these may have a feed-back that is harmful to economic prospects. The classic example of this is Upper Clyde Shipbuilders. Mr Heath's Government undoubtedly underestimated the effect their original decisions would have on Scottish opinion generally, and even on the Scottish economy generally.

The industrial departments of government are presented with specific problems, such as the low level of investment, or the need to promote exports or the failure of the machine tool industry. Although it is easy to see the dangers that intervention can have, this in no way relieves government of the pressure to deal with specific problems as they are presented to them. Industrial policy is based on the persuasive presumption, evidenced by long political experience, that when government is presented with specific problems it will have to attempt to deal with them—however strong its *laissez-faire* instinct may be. Governments will then seek to maximise benefits and minimise costs. They will seek to do most good economically and socially, and least harm by way of slowing the processes of industrial adaptation. This will be a difficult balance to hold, even more due to the uncertainties involved than to the political pressures. Their search may be more thorough if they are subjected to the types of discipline outlined in the last three chapters of this book. But they will act, and their actions should be justified by some calculation of reasonable expectation in the specific case.

The fact that industrial policy has such a modest, pragmatic, role has not yet made sufficient impact on the terminology in which political parties present their philosophies of government–industry relations. It is because of the belief that within industrial policy lies the secret not just of faster growth but of faster growth during the life of one parliament, that there has been a propensity to announce great new policy departures, great new principles to set up against old and discredited principles, the white-hot technological revolution against *laissez-faire*, a new and more logical industrial structure against the lassitude and incoherence of the market. By contrast, when industrial policy is seen to fail in these great purposes, the opposite is then claimed to be true, that growth will come from disengagement. The propagation of such great new departures discredits itself by their failure to achieve great effects.

The contribution to economic growth even of the most constructive aspects of industrial policy will always be impossible to disentangle. Industrial policy works alongside market forces. It is merely one of a number of factors determining the competitiveness of a nation's industry. Its success is inevitably dependent on the success of demand management policies. Industry above all wants the prospect of expanding and profitable demand. If governments can offer that prospect, perhaps by a combination of fiscal and exchange rate policies, and preferably do it without too great cycles in the course of expansion and without generating too much inflation, then it may have a favourable effect on the rate of economic growth. If they cannot offer it, nothing else will substitute for it. Governments cannot push industry forward by bits and pieces of aid if industry is not simultaneously being pulled forward by expanding demand for its products.

Industrial policy depends for its success on the environment in which it is expected to work.

Whether the economic system works efficiently or inefficiently it has been found necessary, with the advancing demand for a more civilised way of life, for the State to protect those whom the system does not protect, to control or disperse the concentrations of private power which the system creates, above all to emphasise by its surveillance and intervention that the system should be the servant and not the master of society. The State intervenes in an attempt to make the chance product of the operation of market forces into something rationally defensible in terms of the interest of its people.

But the manner of intervention is important as well as the objective. The market, activated by market forces, may be likened to a computer activated by a highly complex programme. The programme may not yet be perfect, it may not yet meet every need. But it may well be better gradually to improve it than to start again from scratch. Indeed an attempt to start again from scratch may lead to collapse rather than to progress. In so far as possible it is right calculatedly to use and to modify market forces to achieve the objects in mind. One can, for example, achieve something of a devaluation effect in development areas. Investment incentives and the regional employment premium did precisely that and therefore can be regarded as instruments which modify the operations of market forces in a calculated manner, the one to increase investment and the other to encourage the movement of employment to the depressed regions. Planned interventions can then be added at specific points to compensate for the defects that remain in the operation of the market.

The state exists, therefore it intervenes. But it does not have to intervene like a bull in a china shop.

3. *The Public Interest*

Industrial policy is one aspect of the process whereby the State attempts to inject the public interest into the operation of market forces. The concept of industrial policy would thus seem to require some definition of the public interest. Unfortunately, whereas it is possible to illustrate one person's or one government's view of the public interest it is seldom possible to define it in advance of the consideration of specific issues. Some of the studies in this book illustrate the Labour Government's view of the public interest.

The public interest will certainly not be viewed identically by governments of different political parties. Fortunately there is likely to be a considerable concurrence among human beings on whether or not a view of the public interest is being taken honestly, just as it would not be difficult to get widespread agreement among a large number of separate individuals that it is more important to haul back a child who is running into a moving motor car than to catch a halfpenny that is falling through a hole in one's pocket.

There is a rationalistic view that the public interest can be reduced to propositions in economic welfare. According to this view, an attempt should be made to measure all of the costs and benefits to society, and a more rational view can then be taken as to how far it is in the interests of society to protect the weak or improve the regions, how much should be spent on saving human life through safety improvements, better medical care, and so on. However even those who would press this kind of approach furthest, would agree that many costs and benefits are not in fact measurable.

They would agree also that sometimes the answer is so obvious that no formal estimate is necessary, and they would think it not worthwhile to conduct an elaborate study where the social costs of a wrong decision appear to be trivial. Nevertheless there are cases where it is sensible and useful to use a calculus of cost and benefit, and where even the creation of such a framework for thought improves understanding. But cost-benefit analysis is seldom so persuasive that it eliminates the need for judgment; rather it directs attention to those aspects of a problem where judgment is necessary, and it allows the implications of alternative judgments to be assessed with greater clarity and precision. In principle macro-economic policies should also be seen within the framework

48 POLITICAL RESPONSIBILITY AND INDUSTRY

of cost and benefit to society, even though the techniques of cost-benefit analysis are applied more usually in the economic appraisal of projects or of other micro-economic decisions.

As the public interest is a matter of judgment and frequently involves a difficult balance of considerations, personal and governmental assessments of it are not likely to be unanimously agreed or consistent over time. For example the achievement of a faster rate of growth has long been considered as important in the public interest. Yet no one could say that in this country's recent economic history, economic growth has been allowed priority over interests which have been thought to conflict with it, such as the containment of inflation or that we pay our way in the world at a certain exchange rate. The public interest in economic growth is now being questioned in a different sense. Certain types of economic growth are thought to conflict with environmental objectives and sometimes with a sensible conservation policy for resources. Regional policy may in certain of its aspects conflict with priority for economic growth. What is demanded these days by critics of this country's growth rate is a 'higher' priority for economic growth. The relativity of the word 'higher' accepts that there cannot be an overriding public interest even in economic growth, though it does continue as an outstanding important objective of policy and one which humanity, whether in the developed or less developed countries, is clearly not prepared to renounce at this point of time.

There are those who argue that there is a public interest in the uninhibited operation of the profit motive. Mr John Davies, the once philosopher subsequently king of British industry, has said that 'The aggregation of profit [produced] that accretion to total wealth [which is] a principal objective of national or international policy.'[5] He then went on at once to cancel out the significance—if any—of what he had said by adding: 'I do not say "the principal objective" for it too must be reconciled with parallel objectives of political, moral,

[5] International Conference on Monopolies, Mergers and Restrictive Practices, Cambridge, 1969, ed. J. B. Heath (HMSO) p. 33

cultural and other consequence.'[6] In short Mr Davies having marched his audience up the hill to view that original clear insight into the public interest, at once marched them down the hill to contemplate the old, difficult and murky business of attempting to reconcile one objective with another. Indeed as Mr Davies has since been involved in the negotiation on behalf of government of a prices and incomes policy he may now consider the 'aggregation of profit' as worthy of somewhat less emphasis than he did in September 1969.

The 'aggregation of profit' as an absolute objective would also be inconsistent with the preservation of competition. Yet it is widely accepted that there is a public interest in competition and indeed that governments should be as interested in promoting competition as industrialists are supposed to be in maximising profits.

Despite the dangers, there will be occasions when the rescue of lame ducks is seen to be in the public interest. It should not be imagined that government can allow major failures, with the attendant redundancies, out of devotion to abstract principles as to how national good is likely to be maximised. The political and economic effects of major failures are both equally the legitimate concern of government. People will less and less accept that the faults of others should cast them into irremedial redundancy. The real problem in such operations is to ensure that government has a clear objective and that it has designed its intervention in a way which is likely to achieve it.

Legislation frequently enacts statutory definitions of the public interest. It tends to do so in relatively sharply defined situations. There is a rather clear public interest in the prevention of crime, or that consumers should not be deceived or drugs misused. The Restrictive Trade Practices Act 1956 created a presumption that restrictive trade practices in the supply of goods is contrary to the public interest. It said simply that 'A restriction accepted in pursuance of any agreement shall be deemed to be contrary to

6 ibid.

the public interest.'[7] This was however followed by a list
of exceptions to that presumption which slightly complicated
even that straightforward determination. The Monopolies
and Restrictive Practices (Inquiry and Control) Act 1948
attempted in Section 14 to define the public interest in the
circumstances of competition policy generally. The definition
was so general that Professor G. C. Allen has said: 'I do not
remember in the course of my twelve years experience on the
Monopolies Commission that we ever referred to the "Public
Interest" clauses to guide us in our decisions and deliberations.
They really offered no help whatever.'[8]

In 1970 the Labour Government proposed to create a
Commission for Industry and Manpower which was to be
an amalgam of the Monopolies Commission and the National
Board for Prices and Incomes. The project was aborted by the
General Election. In the Commission for Industry and Manpower Bill there appeared in Clause 31 an extended statement
of the matters to which the Commission would have had to
have regard in determining whether actions of companies referred to it operated or might be expected to operate against
the public interest. This clause was put in in an attempt to meet
objections from the CBI (Confederation of British Industry)
to what was felt to be the overwide and under-explicit remit
of the CIM (Commission for Industry and Manpower). It
cannot really be claimed that Clause 31 was very specific. The
Commission was to take account of such matters as efficiency,
economy, quality, productivity, the encouragement of new
enterprises and new investment, the expansion of the market,
and the relationship between increases in income and the
growth of output that would ensure greater stability of prices
and a share of increased efficiency for the consumer. All this
was no doubt very relevant to a determination of the public
interest in industrial situations. The Commission might even
have been aware of them without benefit of the clause. It
hardly tied the hands of the Commission very substantially
in coming to their own view of the public interest, and in any

[7] Section 21
[8] Quoted in the Control of Monopoly–Industrial Policy Group Paper no. 8
p. 18

case the significance of the whole exercise was substantially undermined by clause 31 (1) which said simply that the Commission 'shall take into account all matters appearing to them to be relevant'.[9]

Yet the fact that the public interest is an elusive concept does not mean that it is a meaningless concept. It should be the final criterion of policy. It is concerned, often inevitably in an *ad hoc* way, with the reconciliation of the many relevant factors and objectives. One value of the concept of the public interest is in its requirement that the whole problem be considered. It is of little use coming to a determination which admittedly leaves out important parts of the problem. A partial view is of little help precisely because the difficult question is the proper relationship between the different aspects of the problem. Every aspect must be placed in its proper relationship with every other aspect as measured by judgment aided by such techniques, such as cost-benefit analysis, as are available. In coming to a judgment of the public interest the attempt should be made to give explicit weight, if necessary qualitatively rather than quantitatively, to each of the considerations involved. As these weightings will in any case be implicit in the making of a particular decision, it is better that if possible they be made explicit so that they can be examined by daylight and perhaps modified by criticism.

In some industrial policy decisions, there will be one over-whelming determinant of the public interest, as, for example, the need to rescue a major British firm such as Rolls Royce or to outlaw restrictive trade practices in the supply of goods. These cases will be of great political importance and will come to ministers for that reason, if for no other. In other industrial policy decisions it will be a great deal more difficult to place all the considerations in their relationship. Ministers will find it difficult in such cases to lay down in advance firm guide-lines for policy. This will not therefore be an area of

[9] The Fair Trading Bill of 1972-73 gives slightly firmer guidance as to the public interest by emphasising 'the desirability of maintaining and promoting effective competition'. But the Commission may still take account of all matters which appear to them relevant.

policy which is easily delegated. It will very frequently be necessary for civil servants to refer to the minister for decisions on particular situations and then, hopefully, to gain such guidance as his individual decisions can be interpreted to give.

In view of the complexity of so many industrial situations and despite the amount of time consumed in resolving them, ministers must not succumb to the temptation to produce oversimplified principles of action in the hope that delegation to the department or to an agency will then be possible. The administration of industrial policy is inevitably a voracious consumer of a minister's administrative capacity.

Chapter 3

COMPETITION AND THE PUBLIC INTEREST

1. *The Pragmatic Way with Competition*

Competition policy is at the heart of industrial policy. Governments since the war have found it necessary to intervene, and to negotiate, in order to promote or preserve competition. At first sight nothing should be easier than to agree the principles by which such interventions should be governed, so strong is the consensus that competition is in the public interest. That hope is, however, rapidly overtaken by the complexity of the subject and by the contrasting aspects of the public interest.

The consumer finds that competition provides him with a wider choice of goods and services. As it is a stimulus to lower costs, it provides him with these goods and services more cheaply. The abolition of resale price maintenance increased the incentive to shop around, although one sees in that fact one cost of competition that may be less welcome. It costs energy to shop around, and some consumers may find the mental comfort of knowing that they are not being over-charged worth more than the advantage of an occasional cheap buy.

Doubts about the benefits of competition arise most forcibly in the minds of those whose employment is threatened by its effects. The coal industry, the railways, the cotton textile industry and the shipbuilding industry have suffered marked declines in employment under the impact of competition. Although the economic system may throw up new employment opportunities, it cannot be certain that such opportunities will appear, particularly in the same area or for the older man. It is in part because of this characteristic of competition that the socialist movement has thought of collective rather than competitive ways of achieving the same ends. These fears emphasise the importance of the creative aspects of competition policy discussed in the next section, concerned as they are with government assistance in the creation of jobs. As a matter of fact, over the last ten years there have been as many fears of loss of employment arising from mergers as from competition.

Many critics of other types of government intervention will nevertheless think that governments are seldom so innocently engaged as when they are promoting or preserving competition. Competition promotes innovation, investment and a more efficient use of resources. Yet there will be doubts arising from the realisation that the real world departs by a considerable margin from a model of perfect competition and from the fact that it is easier to argue an hypothesis about the benefits of competition than actually to calculate them.

The lawyer will know that the public interest in competition is deeply entrenched in the Common Law of England. The grant of monopolies to individuals by the Crown was a source of government revenue in the sixteenth and early seventeenth centuries. It was the subject of one of the earlier confrontations between the prerogative of the Monarch and the Common Law as defended by Parliament. As early as 1624, an Act of James I declared all monopolies to be contrary to the laws of this realm and that they ought to be and 'shall be forever hereafter . . . tried and determined according to the common laws of this realm and not otherwise'.[1] As the judgments of the Restrictive Practices Court have shown, the judges and lawyers of this country have inherited this strong sentiment in favour of competition outside their own trade.

Modern politicians have seen competition as a good political cry. A vigorous competition policy may save them from any suspicion of having accepted the embrace of big business. They have been held back from an unbridled enthusiasm for competition by the links that some of them have with sections of industry which see some advantages in

[1] G. W. Prothero *Statutes and Constitutional Documents, 1559-1625* (OUP, 1913)

restrictive practices, and by a belief shared with many leaders of industry that the tendency of British firms to compete among themselves may weaken them in their more vital competitive battle with the foreigner.

Modern governments have shown only a reluctant enthusiasm for competition. They know that they will be responsible for the economic effects of any intervention they make to preserve or promote competition. This fact may incline them towards caution. They will not wish to base their policy on an over-simple model of a perfectly competitive society. They will be aware of the rigidities and imperfection of competition, that it can destroy as well as stimulate, and that its equitable administration requires the attention of archangels rather than men.

However governments, if they are going to act, need an hypothesis from which action can follow. Such an hypothesis might simply be that certain monopolies and mergers need to be investigated in the public interest. Nothing is foredoomed by the hypothesis. It merely gives entry to an investigation, authorised by the government, into such monopolies and mergers, and it is on the result of the investigation that decisions will be based. The danger with most hypotheses about the economy is that they are either so simple as to be clearly untrue, or so complex that no action can follow from them. Here, in competition policy, is thought to exist an hypothesis which at a small cost in administrative capacity, creates the possibility of beneficial action derived from detailed examination, the recommendations of an expert tribunal, and the government's own judgment of the public interest as apparent in the light of the evidence.

While modern British Governments have been prepared, in the name of competition policy, to instigate pragmatic enquiries of this kind, they have never, except in the limited areas of restrictive trade practices, accepted an absolute commitment to competition. The size of the UK market has been believed not to permit such a commitment. It has been thought that there would be occasions when economies of scale would make inevitable market dominance by a single firm. The complexity of the subject and the fact that the public interest in situations of market dominance, or potential market dominance, has not always been as clear as daylight, have also restrained governments from such a commitment.

Both the main political parties have since the war contributed to the development of competition policy in the UK. A Labour Government passed the Monopolies and Restrictive Practices (Inquiry and Control) Act of 1948, the first Act on the subject since the seventeenth century. It was this Act that made subject to enquiry by a Monopolies Commission,[2] monopolies defined as the supply of at least one-third of the market in the UK, or any substantial part of the UK. When the merger question appeared on the political scene as a result of the ICI bid for Courtaulds in 1962, Labour criticised the absence from British law of any system for the control of mergers. It was thus entirely in character that a Labour Government should have passed through Parliament in 1965 the Monopolies and Mergers Act, a further milestone in the history of British competition legislation. This Act extended the powers relating to monopolies and brought under enquiry at the discretion of the government mergers that would create a monopoly, as defined by statute, or which involved the takeover of £5 million assets or more. The same Labour Government promoted the Restrictive Trade Practices Act of 1968 under which information agreements may be made subject to registration and investigation by the Restrictive Practices Court. Information agreements dealing with prices and with terms and conditions of supply have in fact been called up for registration. Finally, in the Commission for Industry and Manpower Bill in 1970, it was proposed to extend the power of enquiry in the public interest into positions of market dominance as well as of monopoly, and to make mergers subject to enquiry not simply when originally proposed, but retrospectively to see whether the planned benefits had actually been achieved. It is right to emphasise that the two Acts of 1948 and 1965 left to government full discretion as to how far they should be implemented to

2 Then known as the Monopolies and Restrictive Practices Commission.

control monopolies and mergers. Their actual implementation has not been very extensive.

The two great competition Acts of Conservative Governments were the Restrictive Trade Practices Act 1956 by which, subject to certain 'gateways', restrictive practices in the supply of goods were declared contrary to the public interest; and the Resale Prices Act of 1964 which did as much for resale price maintenance. There was a clear presumption of guilt not innocence. These Acts are different in character from the Monopolies and Mergers Acts in that they are enforced by an official, the Registrar of Restrictive Practices and by a Restrictive Practices Court.[3] Their operation therefore does not depend on the energy or discretion of government. It is not open to a gentlemanly government to seek more amenable solutions if the court bans an agreement.

During the years of the Labour Government, when salvation through market forces and competition became the watch-word of Conservative policy, Conservative politicians expressed themselves most freely about the benefits of competition, the need for government intervention to achieve it, and about the dangers of conspiracy by businessmen against competition. Thus for example a member of the present Conservative Government, Mr David Howell, said 'Competition is not a natural phenomenon. It is a phenomenon only maintained by an increasingly sophisticated form of intervention.'[4] Sir Keith Joseph, now a member of Mr Heath's Cabinet, said during a series of speeches dedicated to a discussion of government relations with industry: 'Left to themselves, most businessmen would share the market and keep newcomers out.'[5] Thus at that time, whatever the complexity of the considerations, there was no doubt about the declared dedication of the Conservative Party to the virtues of competition.

Industrialists also proclaim the economic advantages of

[3] Under the Fair Trading Bill, introduced in the 1972-73 session of Parliament, the functions of Registrar are taken over by a Director General of Fair Trading.

[4] House of Commons Official Report, 3 December 1969, vol. 792 col. 1647

[5] Conservative Central Office press handout

living in a competitive ambience. They assert that competition helps to keep them and their staff on their toes. They do not quite understand, so it sometimes appears, that the promotion of competition and the maximisation of profit are objectives which may be inconsistent with one another, and therefore not to be spoken of even in after-dinner speeches as though the one is a condition of the other. This apparent confusion does not necessarily mean that businessmen are naïve. It may simply mean that they understand something rather different when they speak about competition. The real question is whether a competitive situation is one promoted, as Mr David Howell put it, by ever more sophisticated forms of government intervention; or whether it is one in which market forces are allowed the freest possible play and in which the role of government is kept to the absolute minimum. It is not surprising to find that when industrialists praise the virtues of a competitive ambience, they are speaking of a situation in which the determination of the public interest is left to the accidental or calculated consequences of their own actions, and in which the role of government is reduced to that of an inactive umpire.

There is no doubt that industry has not liked competition policy as it has developed since the war. The FBI (Federation of British Industries), the predecessor of the CBI, and the Trade Associations, bitterly opposed the 1956 Restrictive Trade Practices Act. Indeed such was the hostility that the Act might not have passed had it not been for seven 'gateways' or statutory justifications for restrictive practices, which were introduced into the Act. Industry and those Tory MPs linked with the Trade Associations hoped that the gateways would let all but the worst restrictive practices through. In fact the Restrictive Practices Court was in its early years very difficult to persuade. Most of the gateways were locked fast by the Court and those few which remained on the latch were passed only on a very few occasions. The Court thus proved to be a savage and almost indiscriminate destroyer of those types of restrictive agreement that could be referred to it. For this reason industry generally has remained hostile to this Act, both to the presumption that restrictive trade practices are contrary to the public interest and to the judicial process for determining whether particular restrictive agreements should be permitted to pass any of the gateways. If they have to choose between evils, businessmen prefer to negotiate with governments about their bad habits, rather than see them fall under the ban of a Court.

Small firms make strong objection to the Restrictive Trade Practices Acts because they regard the restrictive agreement as a method of achieving what large firms achieve by mergers. The Bolton Committee on Small Firms said this:

> Thus if the Monopolies legislation cannot be invoked unless one-third of the market in question is held by one company, and if a merger does not have to be reported for examination by the DTI unless assets worth at least £5 million are to be taken over we can see no reason in equity why combinations of small firms within these limits should be subject to any greater restrictions. We have formed this view and still hold it despite the undoubted belief of officials of the DTI and the Registrar's Office to the contrary. It may well be that the present monopoly legislation is too lenient—we tend to believe that it is—but we cannot see that this justifies unequal treatment of the small firm because it is caught in the meshes of a different Act.[6]

Thus the Restrictive Trade Practices Acts have been thought of as impacting particularly on small firms, and it has been noticed that the enforcement of competition legislation against larger firms and against mergers has not been remarkably active.

Despite this low level of activity, industry has developed a series of arguments to show that government intervention in this field is even less necessary and less desirable than government in practice has thought it to be. The CBI professes to believe that it is a function of government to encourage competition but that government should concern itself only with matters of 'real economic significance'. The Industrial Policy Group, which brings together the chairmen of some

[6] *Report of the Committee of Inquiry on Small Firms* (HMSO) p. 291

of the country's largest companies, has suggested that the only question with which a body such as the Monopolies Commission need be concerned is whether 'reasonably full play' is being given to competition in each case referred to it. If it is, that should be the end of the matter.[7]

This attempt to reduce the role of government was based on three main arguments: the 'industrial logic' argument, the argument of the continuous technological re-creation of competition, and the international competition argument. The industrial logic argument says that British industry must strengthen itself by mergers and rationalisation in order to compete with large foreign firms. If this argument has merit, there is satisfaction to be derived from the increasing concentration in British industry. The Labour Government was so taken with this argument that it set up a public agency, the Industrial Reorganisation Corporation to promote mergers. This episode is discussed later in this chapter. The IRC was not entirely popular with British industry, especially in its earlier days, and its creation led the IPG to argue that perhaps the importance of structure and of industrial logic had after all been exaggerated. Indeed, as with fashions of all sorts, fashionable thinking changes and industrial logic is today less fashionable, though, no doubt on some principle or other, the merger movement actively continues.

The technological argument says that competition is continuously re-created without governments having to bother about it, by technological developments in the form of new products and processes. There is no doubt that this is true, and indeed, it is fortunate that the preservation of competition does not depend only on governments. Nevertheless governments are entitled to ensure, if they can, that this process of continuous technological re-creation is not inhibited by errors of omission or commission. There is no law as to the industrial structure, or intellectual ambience, that best promotes technological innovation. Professors Donald Turner and Oliver Williamson have seen a tendency for large firms to become bureaucratic in their internal organisation and behaviour and to become more conservative over time,

7 Industrial Policy Group *The Control of Monopoly* (Paper no. 8) p. ii

whereas small firms may be more flexible and adaptable to changing circumstances.[8] Christopher Freeman finds that some large firms deliberately attempt to simulate the smaller firm conditions in their own organisation as an innovator. According to this view, it is at the development stage rather than at the innovative stage that the advantages of the large firm with its greater resources appear. Therefore a takeover of a small firm with a good idea may at that stage promote innovation.[9] In 1972 there was a sharp disagreement between the Monopolies Commission and the Chemical Industry EDC. The Monopolies Commission found that a merger of Glaxo with Boots or Beecham would be contrary to the public interest on the ground that either would have a deleterious effect on the level of research and development in the pharmaceutical industry. The EDC on the contrary emphasised the advantages of size for research and development in the pharmaceutical industry. These are all of them questions in which no single judgment can be appropriate to all circumstances. They do not seem questions that market forces are well equipped to determine. Where experts differ, the shareholder confronted with a merger proposal is not in a very good position to decide one way or other. To refer such matters to experts does at any rate appear one step better than the lottery of the market. The technological argument does not therefore seem to end with government out of the arena but very much in it, if it can provide the necessary expert agency.

The third and most powerful argument against over-anxiety in governments as to their responsibilities for the preservation of competition is the international competition argument. It has been increasingly argued in recent years that the liberalisation of international trade, together with the formation of common markets and free trade areas, makes concern about monopoly at home less justified, and argues against competition policies that limit their concern to national producers and sellers of goods and services.

[8] International Conference on Monopolies, Mergers and Restrictive Practices, Cambridge 1969 (HMSO) pp. 15-16, 127ff., 145ff.
[9] ibid.

It is undoubtedly true that in prosecuting a competition policy the facts of international competition must be recognised. Nevertheless it is noteworthy that the USA—the most prosperous common market in the world—has found it desirable to take action against mergers which affect competition not just in the USA as a whole but in significant regional markets. These regional markets can be quite small, certainly smaller than the UK. The British legislation also speaks of monopoly not just within the UK as a whole but in substantial parts of it.

Generally speaking it is easier to transport goods than services, and therefore monopolies in services can be established within the freest international markets. Even with goods there are inhibitions on trade which make international competition an insufficiently reliable guarantor of competition in national markets. There are still tariffs, though reduced. There are still non-tariff barriers. There is inertia, a powerful protective device for any national supplier who has in his relations with his customer the advantages of language, national sentiment, tradition and stocks and services close at hand. There are also industrial practices that limit international competition. There is international price leadership. There are agreements explicit or implicit not to undercut prices. 'If you ruin my home market, I will ruin yours.' There have been cases of simultaneous increases in prices that have not escaped the attention of the High Court of the European Communities. There would be more reason for confidence in international trade as a protection against the abuse of market power if international trade was subject to better international regulation. Thus the international competition argument will undoubtedly be strengthened by entry into EEC, though only at the cost, as far as industry is concerned, of regulation from Brussels and the High Court in Luxembourg under articles 85 and 86 of the Treaty of Rome. Even this should not however prevent British governments looking after their own, while remembering that international trade *is* a relevant consideration in assessing the competitive situation in any particular case.

What businessmen are really saying when they refer to

international competition is that it should be regarded as different in kind from domestic competition. If it is necessary, in order to fight off international competition, to permit mergers and positions of market dominance in the UK, then governments should accept that fact. There is no doubt that from the point of view of British government, international competition is a different animal. The first object of British government has to be to look after British interests including British industry. But there may be various ways in which this task can be fulfilled. There are benefits as well as costs from international competition. British businessmen may lose markets at home but they may gain the availability of large markets abroad. The British consumer gains the advantage of wider choice and perhaps lower price. It is a question of balance and governments are entitled to examine where the balance lies; to defend British interests, but not simply to accept that British interests are necessarily best promoted by permitting the establishment of ever more positions of market dominance within the UK.

There is a special problem regarding the nationalised industries. They have been established by Parliament in the presumed public interest. They are subject to investigation by government and by the Select Committee on Nationalised Industries, and often by consumer councils of one kind or another. They then find that in recent years governments have thought it right to meet public dissatisfaction—particularly with price increases—by subjecting them to enquiry by bodies such as the National Board for Prices and Incomes (NBPI) and the Monopolies Commission. The CIM Bill specifically included the nationalised industries within the scope of reference. The nationalised industries therefore have even more reason than private industry to complain about the cost in management time and energy of these continual investigations. In this they have had the sympathy, but not the practical co-operation, of governments.

Small firms see these problems differently from the great firms that dominate British industry. In certain respects they would like more not less intervention by government. The

Bolton Committee recommended that: 'The Department of Trade and Industry should give consideration to the possibility of referring to the Monopolies Commission the question of the market power exercised by large firms through their buying policies, and the possible damage to the competitive structure of industry, through discrimination against small firms, which results from it.'[10] This is not a recommendation that is likely to commend itself to the IPG.

There were three periods in the history of the Labour Government's competition policy. The first was that of the Monopolies and Mergers Act 1965. This period may be regarded as a hangover from the ICI–Courtaulds merger proposal and from the Conservative Government's 1964 White Paper on competition policy. A Bill in draft in the Board of Trade was taken, was somewhat improved, and was passed in the first few months of the 1964 Parliament. The second period is that of the IRC discussed later in this chapter. The Labour Government proposed to do better what industry was doing for itself to its own entire satisfaction.

The third period was that of the counter attack. Early in 1969, Anthony Crosland as President of the Board of Trade decided to refer to the Monopolies Commission two major mergers, Unilever–Allied Breweries and Rank–de la Rue, neither of which involved the creation of a monopoly, as defined by statute. The references were made explicitly with the intention of cooling the merger-mania of that time. The Monopolies Commission concluded that the Unilever–Allied Breweries merger would not be against the public interest, though it was obvious that the Commission had not been able to detect any significant benefit in it either. But since the Monopolies and Mergers Act contained no presumption in favour of competition, simply a requirement to assess mergers in terms of the 'public interest', the Commission felt unable to find against a merger in which they could see no positive harm. The merger did however fall through, due among other matters to changes in market prices between the time of the

10 *Report of the Committee of Inquiry on Small Firms* (HMSO) p. 299

two companies' original agreement and the permissive report of the Monopolies Commission. A merger so keenly advocated in December could not overcome such obstacles in June.

The Commission did find the Rank–de la Rue merger against the public interest on the ground that its effect on the staff of de la Rue would seriously reduce the efficiency of the merged company. This conclusion was much criticised at the time. It was argued that if such matters were to be considered relevant to a Monopolies Commission enquiry, the staff of any company could defeat a takeover bid by professing anxiety or an intention to leave if the takeover was consummated. More mature reflection has led at least some of the critics to the conclusion that the effect on staff is a relevant consideration in a merger.

Anthony Crosland's counter-attack was reinforced by a study 'General Observations on Mergers' which the Monopolies Commission published as an annex to its reports on these two mergers. The annex drew attention to the need for more information as to the effects of mergers and to the danger constituted by the disappearance of so many independent decision centres in industry. It concluded: 'there is no reason to think that this merger activity has so far led to the growth of companies whose absolute size is such as to raise important questions for the public interest. It is however leading to the continued absorption of medium sized companies not necessarily accompanied by gains in efficiency.'[11]

Contemporary with these two references was the Textile Structure Enquiry of which an account is given later in the chapter. The final episode in the counter-attack was the CIM Bill, which would have had the effect of strengthening competition law in an attempt to find in competition some substitute, though obviously an inadequate substitute, for the dying prices and incomes policy.

The CIM Bill failed through the change in government in June 1970. A Conservative Government came to power dedicated to competition policy as its proclaimed priority,

[11] The Monopolies Commission *The Rank Organisation Ltd and the De La Rue Company Ltd* (HMSO) p. 56, para. 35

and then took two and a half years to decide what exactly its competition policy should consist of.[12]

What has emerged from all these changes of emphasis, these conflicting pressures and trends, these cross-currents of argument and counter argument? The inevitable result is pragmatism. Within the pragmatism there is an area of principle, the principle enshrined in the 1956 Act that restrictive practices in the supply of goods are contrary to the public interest. Some element of pragmatism has been inserted even here as, under the Restrictive Trade Practices Act of 1968, it is open to the government to give temporary exemption from registration to restrictive agreements of substantial importance to the national economy. As a matter of fact this power has been little used because little need has so far been shown. But in the great area of monopolies, mergers and market dominance, the attitude is pragmatic. The government will make a reference if it is worried. It is then up to the companies or industry referred to prove their case before an administrative tribunal known as the Monopolies Commission,[13] consisting of good men and true, men whose background in the law, industry or academic life is believed to make them appropriate assessors of the public interest. If they find things done or the danger of things being done against the public interest, they will so report. The government will then make its own assessment of the public interest, consult with the parties, and hand down its determination within the very considerable powers open to it on a public interest finding by the Commission.

This pragmatism is clearly right in UK circumstances. Decisions of this importance cannot be contracted out to a Court because it is government that will be responsible for the consequences of any decision, and where they are as significant as they may well be in the case of some monopolies and mergers, it is sensible that this government discretion should be retained.

[12] The Fair Trading Bill was introduced in December 1972.
[13] Under the Fair Trading Bill, to be known as the Monopolies and Mergers Commission.

There have, however, been doubts about the actual operation of the pragmatic way with competition.

First, pragmatism means uncertainty. No one knows why some monopolies and mergers are referred for enquiry and others not. Indeed governments have been known to change their minds. When Beecham bid for Glaxo at the end of 1971, the government decided not to refer, having taken the view that such a merger would not be contrary to the public interest. But when Glaxo fixed up a defensive merger with Boots, the government threw the whole problem at the Monopolies Commission, the Beecham bid as well as the Boots bid. The Monopolies Commission found both contrary to the public interest. There is thus reason to doubt whether the public interest is in fact adequately safeguarded by rapid reviews by a mergers panel in the Department of Trade and Industry, subject, in important cases such as this, to ministerial approval, which lead to a decision whether or not to refer a proposed merger to the Monopolies Commission.

The government determines what references it shall make.[14] The Commission determines the public interest in the reference. The government finally determines whether it should act on any finding by the Commission that things are being done, or that a merger might be expected to operate, against the public interest. It is not surprising that inconsistency has been detected in the approach both of the Monopolies Commission and of successive governments to particular monopolies or mergers.

The pragmatism extends to the determination of the public interest. The IPG has said that the Monopolies Commission should not concern itself with such elusive concepts as the 'public interest'.[15] Interestingly enough the IPG gives as an example of a misguided Monopolies Commission Report that to which we refer later in this chapter, the Report on Manmade Cellulosic Fibres. The IPG comments that 'It would be difficult to conceive of a more highly competitive situation',[16]

[14] Under the Fair Trading Bill, monopolies, but not mergers, may be referred by the Director-General.

[15] *The Control of Monopoly*, op. cit., p. ii

[16] ibid. p. 23

but as the account of the Textile Structure Enquiry will show, issues of a competition policy can be more complex than the IPG allows. However competitive the situation in which Courtaulds found itself, what the government there faced was a head-on clash between two major companies which might have had an effect on the investment policy of one of them which could have been harmful to the country's economy. That elusive concept 'the public interest' could not have been more clearly involved. This case does illustrate the reality of the public interest as a concept against which particular competitive situations may have to be considered. There are indeed many other public interest factors which can appropriately be considered in judging a merger or monopoly— the effect for example of their activities on employment in development areas.

It is interesting that Arthur Knight, the Deputy Chairman of Courtaulds (not a member of the IPG), in his companion volume in this series[17] has no doubt that the public interest is a valid concept against which to judge mergers and positions of market dominance. The question has been not whether the concept of the public interest should be abandoned but whether some further guidance should be given by Parliament, for example by way of enacting a presumption in favour of competition and by stating clearly that social factors such as the desirability of promoting a balanced distribution of industry in the UK are a legitimate element in the assessment of the public interest by both government and Monopolies Commission.

The next problem is what gathering of archangels could be capable of determining the public interest in monopolies and mergers, even with further guidance from Parliament. The answer is that the Monopolies Commission is not a heavenly host. But the judgment of experienced people who have no private interest in the matter and who are able to seek out the relevant information is the most practical method available. The alternative is to leave these questions to the chances of market forces and to shareholders. Market forces are an

[17] A. Knight *Private Enterprise and Public Intervention: The Courtaulds Experience* (Allen & Unwin 1973)

expression of power, not necessarily of the public interest. Shareholders are primarily concerned with their own private interests. They are, moreover, likely to be ignorant of many material matters. Indeed the subsequent comments of chairmen of companies, explaining why they have been unable to achieve the success anticipated out of the mergers they have carried through, illustrate how often even chairmen are ignorant of many material matters. Ignorance is not the most useful of market forces, nor does it provide the most persuasive way of determining the public interest.

The IPG suggested that the Monopolies Commission should not look upon itself as a kind of supreme management consultancy agency. This sarcasm underlines an understandable tendency among the industrialists of the IPG to believe that if they are allowed to have their way, the public will benefit, industrial efficiency will be enhanced, and competition will not be prejudiced. But as these eminent gentlemen should be only too well aware, giants may sleep as well as compete. Difficult as the question may be, the Monopolies Commission is certainly entitled to investigate what effect a particular merger, for example, is likely to have on the competitive strength of the merged company. The administrative problems of squeezing out of the merger the advantages that allegedly should follow from it have again and again been found to be very great.

Arthur Knight shows that he prefers the procedures and style of the NBPI to those of the Monopolies Commission. He accepts however that the NBPI had precise guide-lines whereas the Commission dealt with the much vaguer concept of the public interest. He thinks that it might be possible to formulate clearer guide-lines for the Commission to follow. This is something all governments have found it impossible to do if the pure pragmatic way with competition was to be retained. The only step that could be taken would be to introduce some presumption in favour of competition. The effect of such a presumption, which would have to be far more conditional than the presumption in the Restrictive Trade Practices Act, is discussed below. Certainly it would not eliminate uncertainties in regard to a public interest determination. It would slightly restrict the area of uncertainty.

He also believes that a department on the lines of that of the Registrar of Restrictive Trade Practices should be set up and that it should have the task of presenting the case to the Commission. Under the Fair Trading Bill of 1972-73, the Government of Mr Heath proposes to create a post of Director-General of Fair Trading. He takes over the job of Registrar of Restrictive Trade Practices. In addition he will be the government's expert on questions of competition. He will have the right, subject to ministerial veto, to refer monopolies, but no right to refer mergers, but he may recommend to the Secretary of State that a certain merger should be referred. He is not however an arbiter of the public interest. In the case of restrictive trade practices, the judgment remains with the Court and the Director's power of reference is strictly controlled by statute. In the case of monopolies and mergers, decisions as to the public interest remain matters for the Commission and for the government. The Bill sensibly refrains from asking Parliament to lay down, in the case of monopolies and mergers, binding criteria for the determination of the public interest. Thus the Bill continues in the British tradition of the pragmatic way with competition. The government retains its power over decisions which may be of considerable economic and social importance. It is right that it should be so. From this point of view it will be necessary for the British government to watch very carefully the actual operation of Article 86 of the Treaty of Rome under which positions of market dominance in inter-state trade within EEC can be the subject of enquiry by the Commission and reference to the High Court of Luxembourg.

The pragmatic way with competition does have many problems. Nevertheless they are worth living with for the sake of a workable competition policy. Without departing too far from pragmatism, it would however be desirable to strengthen competition policy in the following three ways. First there should be a government decision to refer to the Monopolies Commission all major mergers unless there is a very clear reason why not. Mergers between large companies do involve

the public interest and deserve attention not just by shareholders, but by the government and the Monopolies Commission on behalf of the public as a whole. The complexity
and importance of the considerations involved suggest that
it is inappropriate in effect to leave the determination of the
public interest in these matters to shareholders. At the very
least such references would lead to disclosure of material facts
which do not become public in the course of a takeover that
is left simply to the arbitrament of the market. Secondly there
should be provision for greater disclosure by merged companies of the results achieved by merging. This should be
regarded as part of competition law rather than of company
law.

Thirdly it should make for a more effective surveillance of
monopolies and mergers if Parliament were to depart from
neutrality so far as to enact a general presumption in favour
of competition. The object would be to guide ministers and
the Commission. It would mean that in cases where the
Commission could not identify either positive harm or positive benefit, it would find in favour of competition. Such a
presumption would slightly move the point of balance in a
decision as to the public interest. In a merger it would be
necessary to show benefit and not simply that there would
be no harm. One result might be that the Commission would
have found against the Unilever–Allied Breweries merger.
Parliament would define gateways limiting the presumption.
It would, for example, say that in assessing the competitive
situation regard should be had to the need to promote
technical or economic progress while allowing consumers a
fair share of the resulting benefit. But there would have to
be clear gains to set against any sacrifice of competition.
Clause 79 of the Fair Trading Bill, the 'public interest'
clause, directs the Commission in assessing the public interest
to take account, among other things, of 'the desirability of
maintaining and promoting effective competition'. It may be
that these words will achieve what is necessary. We will have
to see.

Nevertheless, though with these modifications, it is sensible
that the element of discretion in the approach to monopolies

and mergers should continue. Despite the acclaim given to competition, the public interest in industrial situations is frequently difficult to identify and can seldom be determined in advance by dogmatic principles. There is the danger that if discretion is left with government, arrangements will be cooked up which conciliate businessmen rather than protect the public interest. But this is an inevitable effect of any decision to be pragmatic, and pragmatism tinged with principle in the way described above is still the better approach to the regulation of monopolies and mergers in the context of the UK economy. Despite its dislike of the discretionary element in references, industry is likely to approve the idea that government should retain a discretion as to how far it goes in implementing the conclusions of a Monopolies Commission Report. Some protection against the smoke-filled room can be provided if the Monopolies Commission were encouraged to comment publicly on any arrangements made by government in implementation of its report.

2. *The Creative Way with Competition*

From a presumption in favour of competition, another more controversial proposition follows. The Italian economist Pasquale Saraceno has argued that a prime function of IRI, the Italian State Holding Company, is to strengthen competitive forces in the Italian economy. According to Saraceno the State should supplement private initiative and increase the efficiency of market mechanisms by direct intervention through an instrument such as IRI.[18]

Proposals by the Labour Party for the creation of a State holding company in Britain derive in large part from the example of IRI. Some of the activities of IRC, by strengthening companies in which they took an interest, had a positive effect on the competitive situation. There are many ways in which a government may directly promote competition. Support to the British computer industry promoted competition against the mammoth and dominant IBM. The rescue of Rolls Royce sustained competition against the American

[18] Stuart Holland (ed.) *The State as Entrepreneur* (Weidenfeld & Nicolson) pp. 5-7

aero-engine manufacturers. Regional policy with the special assistance it provides for new industrial activities in development areas may strengthen competitive forces nationally. The government can speed innovation if it is prepared to help with industrial research and development. As the important factor here is not that research should be done but that its results should be used, research and development contracts with industry are likely to be more productive than somewhat isolated research in government laboratories. It was Lord Blackett who said that one qualified scientist or engineer in industry was worth three in a government laboratory. Competition, and hence the better working of the market, may be promoted by new investment. Investment incentives which may influence the level of investment are therefore from this point of view a weapon of competition policy. It was a curiosity in a Conservative government so wedded, in words at least, to competition, that by reintroducing tax allowances as the principal investment incentive they should have weakened competitive forces. Tax allowances strengthen the strong and weaken the weak because they are most valuable to those who have had the profits against which they can be set. They also build up in unprofitable firms and become an enticement to takeover bids for which there is no industrial justification. Investment grants, on the contrary, not being profit-related are a much better instrument to promote competition.

Government action which has the effect of creating competition will, whether or not that is its principal object, always be held unfair by established industry. IBM regarded as unfair the favour shown by successive governments to ICL, although without that favour ICL could never have hoped to become an effective competitor against IBM. The Lancashire textile industry, which was not in a development area, regarded as unfair the assistance which Courtaulds obtained for its new weaving capacity simply by locating it at Skelmersdale in a development area. British industry generally regarded as unfair the high level of assistance given by British governments to American firms which located themselves in development areas. There is always suspicion that the conduct of subsidiaries of nationalised industries operating ancillary activities will be unfair to their competitors. The activities of a State holding company would certainly be regarded as representing unfair competition.

If fairness is defined as the free operation of market forces, all these activities are certainly unfair. But if there is a public interest in the promotion of competition then it is not possible to say that an activity of government dedicated to the creation of competion is necessarily unfair. It depends on the circumstances of each intervention, and government must retain its discretion.

The desirability of enacting a presumption in favour of competition does not mean that competition policy such as is here described is all that the public interest requires. That fact is recognised in our law which, as amended by the Fair Trading Bill, will make it clear that competition is only one aspect of the public interest. Competition will not substitute for a prices and incomes policy. It will not substitute for a consumer protection policy. It is not a miracle worker whose all-embracing sweep eliminates the need for other policies. It may not satisfy an impatient government nor an impatient public. Yet it works. Though this may depend to some extent on the vigour with which governments activate the regulatory aspects of competition policy, it is likely to be found that from the social point of view, competition will become a more rather than a less disturbing factor in society. This would make even more evident the responsibility of government to assist in the creation of employment and of adequate retraining facilities.

3. *The Industrial Reorganisation Corporation*
Governments are no different from individuals or companies in seeking simple principles by which they can act. The difference lies rather in the size of the resources that governments can put behind their principles. Because governments can commit large resources, they can make big mistakes. Yet it should not be forgotten that large companies too can commit large resources and can therefore make big mistakes. It may

be claimed that at least the latter would be private resources, not public resources. This is an unreal distinction. National resources are lost when they are wasted by a company as they are when wasted by a government.

The fundamental principle which lay behind the creation of the Industrial Reorganisation Corporation was that there was need for more concentration and rationalisation to promote greater efficiency and competitiveness in British industry, and that a government agency could use public money to achieve that end. It was believed that the units of British industry were too small, certainly as compared with the giants of American industry but also as compared with the main exporting sectors of German industry. It was realised that by European standards British companies were large, but that fact was not inconsistent with the idea that production units were too small for optimal economies of scale in production, marketing and research and development. The White Paper (Cmnd. 2889) of January 1966 on the Industrial Reorganisation Corporation said: 'Many of the production units in this country are small by comparison with the most successful companies in international trade ... large groups may often have been built up [in Britain] haphazardly or solely to achieve wide diversification and may not therefore be organised to secure full efficiency ... There is no evidence that we can rely on market forces alone to produce the necessary structural changes at the pace required.'

The scientists and engineers advising government had a particular influence. They calculated the minimum viable size of research and development departments in industry, from that they moved by standard factors to the minimum turnover required to support such a research and development effort and hence to the principle of restructuring British industry. As Lord Blackett said in 1966: 'it is the necessary cost of the R. & D. which determines the minimum necessary output and this determines the minimum size of firm.'[19]

Thus emerged the concept of 'industrial logic'. Industrial

---

[19] Thirteenth Fawley Foundation Lecture *Technology, Industry and Economic Growth* (University of Southampton 1966) p. 11

logic would determine the 'industrial structure which will enable us to make the most effective use . . . of our resources of skill, management and capital'. In the control of takeovers and mergers, the concept would enable the government to distinguish the good from the bad. It was still considered necessary to distinguish the good from the bad. After all there might still be 'haphazard' mergers, or mergers designed 'to achieve wide diversification'.

The IRC accomplished some important mergers. Professor W. G. McClelland, a Director of the IRC, has calculated that: 'In early 1971 it looked as though, out of the 79 projects which IRC had undertaken, 16 were struggling a bit, but no less than 54 had been undoubtedly successful. A score of 8 out of 10 must be regarded as good.' He concedes, however, that this record is 'unconfirmed' and that the time for a final assessment is not yet.[20]

The IRC had other values for the government. It became a source of experience and advice in all manner of industrial situations and thus freed the Civil Service from responsibilities which it feared because it lacked, and knew it lacked, the experience to shoulder them itself. It increased the government's capacity for selectivity in industrial matters. This was a need the Conservative Government was to rediscover after two years of struggling with the consequences of diminishing that capacity by abolishing the IRC. It showed towards the end of its life that it held within itself possibilities for development in other directions, for example as a State holding company or a national investment bank.

Apart from its sponsorship of mergers, it had another value for industry. It recruited many bright and highly articulate young men who subsequently moved straight to senior positions in industry.

The Industrial Reorganisation Corporation did not create the merger mania but it gave it further impetus. Even at the highest point of IRC's activities it influenced only a small proportion of the mergers then taking place, though many of those it sponsored were of major importance. The principle

[20] *Three Banks Review* June 1972 p. 38

of industrial restructuring was in tune with much industrial thinking of the time. What was feared about the IRC was not its stated objective, but the fact that it was a government agency which could use public money to influence the market in directions which the agency rather than the market felt to be good.

'The market' is not an abstraction. It is a place where men of power deploy their resources to achieve their objectives. Naturally such men of power will object when they see a government agency equipped with even larger resources than their own, entering the market and diluting their power. They therefore produce self-interested arguments against the existence of such an agency. Thus the Industrial Policy Group has stated: 'we find no satisfactory evidence to support the view that the relatively slow progress of British industrial productivity in recent years is attributable to major deficiencies in the structure of British industry.'[21] Yet its members did not go on to renounce their own restructuring activities. On the contrary, after emphasising how much concentration had occurred in the British economy in the past without any help from an IRC, they went on to say that the future changes in the structure of industry should 'for the larger part'[22] be left to work themselves out through the decisions of individual companies, such no doubt as their own. In other words they were saying that whether or not there were major deficiencies in the structure of British industry, there were particular mergers that they might promote from which competitive benefits would flow. Nevertheless they wanted no competition from a government agency, they wanted to be left alone in the market place, and as dominating influences in the market place, and they saw no reason at all why governments should deny them that wish. The function of government was to help 'to maintain a generally competitive environment', which is industry's language for telling government to keep out. It will be remembered that the more powerful feudal barons had a not dissimilar view of the functions of government.

[21] Industrial Policy Group *The Structure and Efficiency of British Industry* (Paper no. 6) p. i
[22] ibid. p. ii

It is not surprising that governments have sometimes been unwilling to leave mergers to the market alone. The public interest is very much involved. Important mergers can have important economic and social effects. Competition policy now provides a form of negative control in the public interest. Thus the first question raised by the existence of the IRC was whether in principle a para-governmental agency was capable in a more positive way of injecting the public interest into the operations of the market or whether those operations were to be left simply to the exercise of industrial power subject only to such restraint as competition policy could provide. It has been admitted by the Industrial Policy Group that a large number of the privately sponsored mergers of recent years have failed in their objectives, and other evidence supports this view. They say 'there is no doubt that there are now available improved managerial techniques which should increase the likelihood that mergers will less frequently fall short of expectations'.[23] One suspects that this is merely another example of the optimism which has led the members of the Industrial Policy Group into error in the past and is likely to do so again in the future. But if it is true, the techniques are open for use by a government agency. There is no reason at all to believe that such an agency should be in principle less competent in promoting mergers, if that is what is required, than is private industry. It depends on its method, its motivation and its responsibility.

It is characteristic of men of power that when they find that a new factor has been injected into a situation, they will accommodate themselves to it. The accommodation in this case was very rapid. After all, businessmen who found that they could co-operate with the IRC might thereby be enabled to achieve objectives otherwise far beyond what their own resources could command. A key question in many takeover situations became whether the IRC could be attracted to one's own side. The IRC therefore in the end came to be as much loved as hated. For every victim there was a victor. The IRC was also at least as enthusiastic as any British industrialist to

[23] Industrial Policy Group *Merger Policy* (Paper no. 9) p. 7

achieve what has always been, in the economic difficulties of the 1960s as much as in those of the 1920s and 1930s, the main object of rationalisation schemes: protection through the medium of market dominance.

The second question raised by the existence of the IRC was whether it was right to set up an agency motivated by such a restricted remit. A government agency, publicly financed and inspired by statute with a single, powerful idea, can be very dangerous. It soon appeared that all industrial problems would be analysed and solved in terms of 'structure'. 'Management' was important but 'structure' was more important. For that there was not merely received contemporary wisdom but the Industrial Reorganisation Corporation Act, the fundamental law of the institution. The Act said, it was to 'promote or assist the reorganisation or development of any industry'. It was 'to consider which industries it would be expedient to reorganise or develop' and then 'to seek to promote or assist the reorganisation or development of those industries'. The word 'development' in this quotation from the Act should not be taken to imply that the IRC could of its own volition go beyond reorganisation or restructuring. It could not, for example, simply inject money into a single company. The statutory requirement that IRC reorganise or develop an 'industry' in fact limited its initiative to restructuring. Only if requested by the Secretary of State could it, under section 2 (i) (b), 'establish or develop, or promote or assist the establishment or development, of any industrial enterprise'. Thus, unless it was requested by the Secretary of State, its function was to search for opportunities for industrial restructuring and to promote restructuring when it found such opportunities. In the course of that search the IRC could be rather superficial; but however superficial, it had the money to put where its mouth was.

In the IRC's report for 1968-69 it says:

The key part of IRC's work is its frank and confidential exchanges with individual companies, not just on the nature of the problems facing their industries—important as it is to understand this fully—but also on the practical steps that can be taken towards solving them. IRC is working at close quarters with companies in one industry after another, in seeking improvements in structure and performance.[24]

There is an obvious gap in the argument. Why should the 'practical steps' always involve 'improvements in structure'? Of course they did not, but IRC possessed by statute only one remedy. In *The Doctor's Dilemma* there is a surgeon whose operation for the removal of the (non-existent) nuciform sac is a guaranteed cure for all bodily ills. So it was with Doctor IRC. He had a single cure for all industrial ills.

To whom, and in what respects, was the IRC responsible? The government found that, like Frankenstein, it had little control over its monster. The Industrial Reorganisation Corporation Act guaranteed the IRC's independence, as ministers who had been responsible for drafting the Act were frequently reminded by those they had appointed to run it. It had been hoped that the Corporation's independence of ministerial control would make it more acceptable to industry. In the same interest a highly prestigious board of industrial leaders was appointed to run it. The existence of such a board reinforced its independence of government.

As it became highly activist, it was very attractive to the Press. It developed good Press relations, the more easily because its principle of action was so simple. This popular success reinforced its independence still further.

The functions of the IRC can be stated, generally, as being to inject the public interest into certain industrial situations. This makes it more strange that a body of businessmen should have been given such independence in deciding the public interest. There were two safeguards. The first was that the IRC's money, by way of loan and Exchequer dividend capital, came from the government. The second was competition policy. But ultimate safeguards of this kind, which a government will hesitate to use, are not particularly satisfactory. The real safeguard was the good sense of the members of the IRC. It would have been better if, without denying the

24 IRC Report and Accounts 1968-69 p. 7

IRC a proper degree of independence in action, clear lines of responsibility to government and Parliament had been written into the Act.

The government, in setting up the IRC, never thought through the problem of responsibility. The IRC was not responsible to the government except to the extent that it was to the government that it had to look for its money, and the government expected some return. It could not be held responsible for the short-term effects of its actions because the benefits of these were to be revealed only in the long term. Although it installed directors and appointed managers, it was not really even responsible in the long term because it was not a holding company and was denied the right to hold a long-term equity interest. In any case responsibility in the long term is a very dilute form of responsibility for a body most of whose directors were non-executive and on two-year appointments.

The IRC did not act irresponsibly. Obviously its board would strive to satisfy itself that projects put to it did deserve its support. The board appreciated the need to remain acceptable to the industrial community. Indeed in view of what seemed for most of its life the probability of a Conservative victory at the next general election, it was essential that the IRC should remain acceptable if it was to have any hope of surviving an election. Nevertheless towards the end of its days, it sometimes seemed to claim a prerogative to interfere in industrial policy generally against the wishes of the government. This characteristic did, however, contain the healthier element that in its own process of learning it was beginning to look around for principles of action more sophisticated than the simple principle of merger-making.

No doubt the Labour Government also learnt, and had it been returned to office in June 1970 it might have sought means of both increasing Parliamentary control and of freeing the IRC of its statutory commitment to making mergers.

One advantage of wide general principles, however misguided, is that they enlarge the area within which decision-making is eased by the absence of conflicting principles. Thus if government determines that industry should be restructured at all costs, there is no difficulty at all in accepting whatever ensues, provided perhaps that the proposed restructuring conforms to recognisable industrial logic. But once conflicting principles are allowed to emerge, problems are thrown back into the melting pot. Thus with the rise in unemployment, the IRC was asked to have regard to the employment consequences of its mergers. It promised to do so, but it could not undertake this promise very convincingly because if higher productivity was to be the consequence of the mergers, employment levels might well be threatened. Whether demand expanded sufficiently to absorb the prospective redundancy was not, after all, in the hands of the IRC to determine. The request was even less convincing when it was put to private firms in the form of a code of practice for those involved in mergers. But at any rate one can say that while token regard was paid by all to the principle of minimising redundancy, there was no real conflict with the principle of industrial restructuring because the regard that was paid was only token.

More real was the conflict that was allowed to emerge between the principle of industrial restructuring and the principle of preserving competition. Industrial logic may sometimes be important, but in its relevance to particular situations it needs careful scrutiny. It is not easy to know what is the optimal industrial structure in any particular case. Indeed the optimal industrial structure must necessarily, due to technological changes, be continually changing itself. In any case there is reason to doubt how frequently it was the main motive in a takeover bid. One important reason for the popularity of merger-making at the time was the desire for company growth, especially in industries where demand could be expected to expand only slowly. Since the salaries of top executives tend to be related to company size, this was a peculiarly powerful motivation. Another source of this popularity was to be found in the hope that merger-making would reduce competition. It was essentially a protectionist idea, protectionism through market dominance. This was the case whether the merger was made by the IRC or by the market. The emergence of such an idea is only too comprehensible at a time of declining competitiveness when industrialists are unlikely to commit themselves to achieving economies of scale through export sales especially when they have had long experience of the way governments may seek to support an over-valued currency.

Professor W. G. McClelland has commented: 'IRC sometimes received professional advice suggesting that mergers would be desirable because they would create "a stronger selling position", making possible higher trading margins and a better return on capital.' This line of argument, Professor McClelland says, is in general based on 'the fallacy of equating net profits with the national interest. The fact that it could be propounded so earnestly from quarters of such standing shows how necessary it is to look carefully at the effects of mergers on competition.'[25]

There was no necessary conflict between the principle of industrial restructuring and competition policy as it emerged from the 1965 Monopolies and Mergers Act. The British attitude to monopolies and mergers as enshrined in the Act was pragmatic. It accepted that there might be gains from monopolies and mergers that justified the sacrifice of competition. It was therefore by no means inconsistent in logic to say that mergers promoted by the IRC or by private firms which showed good prospect of economic gain, should be allowed to proceed; but that where there was substantial doubt as to whether the prospective gains justified the sacrifice of competition, the merger in question should be referred to the Monopolies Commission. Only journalists who deal in the very simplest concepts, simpler even than the concept of industrial restructuring, could find this contradictory. Certainly businessmen interested in promoting mergers which might be referred for investigation by the Monopolies Commission would attempt to exploit any suggestion of inconsistency in the government's attitude. But such attempts could have been dealt with easily had the government from the beginning been seen to act on the principle that the creation of the IRC in no way derogated from

25 McLelland *Three Banks Review* June 1972 p. 29

the necessity that mergers must show gains to be set against any loss of competition.

The trouble was that the government went overboard for its new principle of industrial restructuring. 'Structure' became the answer to all industrial problems. Competition became old hat and was thought to be closely linked with *laissez-faire*. The Monopolies Commission was regarded as a collection of fuddy-duddies whose reports, in any case slow in coming, were irrelevant to a modern technological age. As this was known to be the predominant attitude in the government, it did seem surprising when every now and then other principles were forced to the fore.

It may seem odd that a Labour government should pursue policies whose principal effect was to increase the power of a few large private companies. The IRC experience illustrates the power and the danger of a simple, healing, idea at a time of economic siege. But while it provides a warning, it should be taken as a caution against over-simple principles uncritically received, rather than against a more sceptical use of public money to help in the achievement of industrial objectives. A government agency of the right type, with clear lines of responsibility and with the right remit, can have a beneficial role in injecting the public interest into the conflicts of industrialists; a role comparable with that of the government itself, or of agencies such as the NBPI, in injecting the public interest into conflicts between employers and employees or between producers and consumers. The public interest is the government's responsibility and it needs a variety of instruments of intervention to achieve it. It is regrettable that the IRC should have been abolished rather than developed in directions which its potentiality and acquired experience made possible. It is not always necessary to drain off the baby with the bath water.

4. *The Structure Problem in the Textile Industry*
This section recounts how a specific structure problem in the textile industry was managed by the government. It illustrates how even the availability of a detailed analysis by the Monopolies Commission, of the machinery of the 1965 Act to

investigate merger situations, and of the instrument of industrial logic in the IRC proved inadequate or inappropriate, and how pragmatism was in the end bound to prevail.

The textile industry problem may also be of interest because Arthur Knight in his companion volume in this series has written about the identical subject from a quite different point of view. His company—Courtaulds—played a leading role in restructuring the textile industry, and he has written with the perspective of a senior executive intimately involved. I also was personally involved, but as a member of the government.

The cotton textile industry, once Lancashire's pride, had long been in decline. Imports had eaten deep into its domestic market. Its vast export markets had for ever disappeared. With the decline in employment in the industry, its political importance had also declined. But concentrated as so much of it was in Lancashire, and with many thousands of workers still in employment, it remained an industry which could command the attention of government.

The industry was important not only to governments, and to those who worked or had invested their money in it. It was important also to the producers of synthetic fibres. Of these the largest was ICI with its virtual United Kingdom monopoly in the production of nylon and polyester fibre. There was also Courtaulds with a virtual monopoly in the production of cellulosic fibres and a manufacturer too of acrylic fibres, which ICI did not make and in which Monsanto and Dupont were its competitors. In addition to ICI and Courtaulds, some foreign chemical manufacturers produced, or planned to produce, synthetic fibres in the United Kingdom though on a much smaller scale. The textile industry as a whole, including the cotton textile industry, was the principal customer for synthetic fibres which were used not just on their own but in mixtures with wool and cotton. For the synthetic fibre manufacturers therefore the survival of the cotton textile industry was important if they were to retain a UK market for their products. Indeed ICI was concerned not simply as a fibre manufacturer but as a dyestuffs manufacturer and as a supplier of many other chemicals used in the textile industry.

The fibre manufacturers were also a potential source of money for the reorganisation and re-equipment of the cotton textile industry. Indeed they were one of the most hopeful sources. They had large resources which the cotton textile industry itself could not command and they had a strong interest in ensuring its survival. ICI came to see this need to strengthen the textile industry, which was so important as a customer. But its method was to provide finance for restructuring rather than to acquire textile firms itself. In the USA it had been established as a matter of public policy, in fact as an aspect of competition policy, that fibre manufacturers were not permitted to buy up their textile customers. ICI believed this policy to be right in principle, and that vertical takeovers of textile firms by fibre manufacturers should be banned in the United Kingdom too. Although in the special conditions of the UK ICI saw the need to finance companies in the textile industry, and, for example, financed the growth of Viyella, it always insisted that the companies it assisted should and would remain free in their purchasing policy, and unrestricted in their choice of fibres.

Courtaulds too was interested in the survival of its customers. It had the particular problem of a large investment in the manufacture of cellulosic fibres, such as rayon, which were fighting a difficult competitive battle against the newer synthetic fibres. Courtaulds had a very different background of experience from that of ICI. It was not merely a fibre producer. It was by origin itself a textile company and possessed major textile interests. Courtaulds therefore took a view of the link between fibre manufacture and textile manufacture very different from that taken by ICI and other chemical manufacturers who had never themselves been directly involved in the textile industry. Courtaulds, following the policy suggested by its own rather different origins, involved itself more and more deeply in textile processing by means both of major new investments and takeovers. Indeed it possessed a long list of textile companies that were queuing up to be taken over if only Courtaulds could be persuaded. For many existing owners, to be taken over by Courtaulds was an attractive way out of their precarious dependence on an unreliable market.

The activities of ICI were welcome to the government. How could it not welcome activities which were helping to save an industry and employment, and which seemed to attract no criticism from any other part of industry. In the case of Courtaulds, the problem was more complicated. The textile industry had problems and therefore restructuring under the lead of the dynamic Lord Kearton, Chairman both of Courtaulds and the IRC, might seem a great part of the answer. On the other hand, there were complaints arising out of the fact that Courtaulds, unlike ICI, was not merely a supplier to the textile industry but itself a major competitor of many of its textile customers.[26]

In July 1965, before the government had been converted to the principle of restructuring as a solution to industrial problems, Douglas Jay, President of the Board of Trade, had referred to the Monopolies Commission the 'monopoly' in manmade cellulosic fibres. That meant Courtaulds. In December 1967 the Monopolies Commission, untainted by the winds of change, reported that Courtaulds' policy of extensive participation in the textile industry was a thing done for the purpose of preserving its monopoly in manmade cellulosic fibres and might be expected to operate against the public interest. The Commission made recommendations (not binding on the Board of Trade) to deal with this situation. One was that Courtaulds should not be allowed, without the permission of the Board of Trade, to make further acquisitions in any sector of the textile and clothing industries if its share of capacity (or of sales as appropriate) in that sector exceeded a figure laid down by the Board of Trade, or would do so following those acquisitions. Thus the government found itself confronted with a Report from the Monopolies Commission stating in effect that if it consented to further major takeovers by Courtaulds in the textile

[26] Courtaulds actually started to acquire textile companies in 1959 (Gossard). They were well into the process by the time the IRC was formed.

industry it might be permitting action contrary to the public interest.

The government could have ignored the findings of the Monopolies Commission. But there was a great deal of sympathy for the Commission's conclusions. Some companies in the textile industry believed that Courtaulds was discriminating against them, in favour of its own subsidiaries, in the pricing and supply of cellulosic fibres. Moreover ICI saw great danger to its own position in the British market arising from Courtaulds' acquisitions. The customers Courtaulds was acquiring were also ICI's customers. Courtaulds would have the power to influence their purchases. Courtaulds was proposing to make polyester fibre and would have in its subsidiaries tied customers for its product whenever it began production.[27] To ICI, therefore, the Monopolies Commission's Report was also welcome.

In these circumstances the Monopolies Commission's Report was difficult both to implement and to ignore. A year followed during which Courtaulds, despite the Commission's Report, was permitted to make further major acquisitions in the textile industry. In the summer of 1968 Viyella made a bid for English Sewing Cotton, a major unit in the industry. English Sewing Cotton, in order to defend itself against the Viyella takeover, merged with Calico Printers Association to form English Calico. English Sewing Cotton thus saved itself from the embrace of Viyella and its Chairman, Joe Hyman, but only at the expense of paying too much, as they later found, for Calico Printers Association, and of burdening themselves with the immense problem of converting the CPA assets to profitability.

At this stage, in the summer of 1968, there were five major companies in the textile industry: Courtaulds, Viyella, English Calico, Carrington & Dewhurst and Coats Paton, all of them the product of a series of mergers over recent years. In terms of employment these five companies were responsible for about one-third of the weaving and converting output.

Then in January 1969 Courtaulds made a bid for English

[27] Production did not in fact begin until 1972.

Calico. The result was an immediate outcry from the textile industry that Courtaulds must be stopped, and from ICI that if Courtaulds was not stopped it might have drastically to curtail its investment programme for the manufacture of synthetic fibre in Britain. The government, said ICI, should break the link between fibre manufacture and the textile industry. It should be, as in the USA, a matter of public policy that fibre manufacturers must not buy into the textile industry. In this view ICI was supported by the American-owned fibre manufacturing companies in the United Kingdom. The government was now faced by powerful complainants at least one of whom, ICI, had the means of ensuring that its voice was heard over the clamour about industrial restructuring. The government had to decide whether or not to stop Courtaulds.

Courtaulds presumably had thought through the reasons for its bid. It was, it said, merely forestalling a bid for English Calico from the USA, though no one else had detected such a possibility or could say from whom it might come. It could, itself, use English Calico's assets to good effect. Possession of English Calico's American subsidiary, American Thread, would strengthen Courtaulds' drive into the American market. Possession of the textile finishing plants which CPA had brought into English Calico would provide a facility which Courtaulds would otherwise have to duplicate by new investment. There also appeared to be a strategic motive for the bid. Coats Paton, which was an important Courtaulds customer for acrylic fibre, also bought acrylics from du Pont. To secure control over American Thread, a major competitor of Coats Paton, would strengthen Courtaulds' bargaining position in the battle for sales of acrylics.

As Courtaulds made the bid it must be assumed that they wished it to succeed. There were those however who thought that Courtaulds was forcing the hand of the government to decide one way or the other whether it wished Courtaulds to continue its restructuring policy in the textile industry. This view of the motive for Courtaulds' bid seemed to depend in part on varying interpretations in the Press, which may have been inspired, as to Courtaulds' actual intentions. After the government's eventual decision was handed down, Kearton was quoted as describing his bid for English Calico as 'an interesting marginal operation' (*Guardian* 1 July 1969). Indeed a close scrutiny of the Press during the period after the bid, and as far ahead as 1972, will show that there may have been not merely varying interpretations but varying inspirations. The view that the bid was simply an attempt to force the government's hand is also based on a belief that the government could not have allowed Courtaulds' bid to go ahead. That view is inconsistent with the facts and ignores the strongly held opinion within the government as to the industrial advantages of Courtaulds' policy up to that point.

If however Courtaulds was merely attempting to force the government's hand, and was not terribly interested in whether the bid succeeded or not, it was unwise for two reasons. First it roused ICI. Perhaps it did for ICI in this field something of the same service that, seven years earlier, ICI had done for Courtaulds. The full results of rousing ICI were not to be seen for a further year. But to do so could hardly improve Courtaulds' competitive position. Secondly, the government had, after the Monopolies Commission's Report, allowed Courtaulds to continue to strengthen its position with lesser though important acquisitions. Forcing the government's hand was at least as likely to produce a decision unfavourable to Courtaulds as one favourable to it. To do so in the interests of a bid in whose success he was only marginally interested would seem odd for a general as experienced as Lord Kearton. One must therefore assume that, whatever the subsequent and varying reinterpretations of history, the bid was made because it was hoped that it would succeed. It is true that once Courtaulds had seen the strength of the public reaction to the bid, their resolve appeared to weaken and that they then became willing to forgo the merger with English Calico provided their competitors were equally prohibited from taking over English Calico.

There were two government agencies which, on the face of it, were suitable to consider the problem created by the Courtaulds bid. One was the Monopolies Commission. But the previous Report of the Commission showed what it thought about Courtaulds' policy of acquisition and by finding that it might be expected to operate against the public interest, it empowered the Board of Trade to stop further acquisitions. The Board of Trade could hardly refer the matter back to the Monopolies Commission for a second opinion when the Commission had provided a first opinion which had not been acted upon.

The alternative was to refer the whole question to the IRC. Lord Kearton was no longer Chairman of the IRC. He had resigned at the end of December 1968. His resignation would not have prevented suspicion of the IRC's impartiality if the problem had gone to them. This suspicion would have arisen not just from Kearton's recent connection but from the IRC's commitment to mergers. In any case Kearton did not relish having his recent subordinates enquiring into his affairs. There was a further consideration that was decisive. The element of confrontation between two great powers, ICI and Courtaulds, made of it a political situation which only the government could handle, rather than simply an industrial situation suitable for reference to outside agencies such as the Monopolies Commission or IRC. The problem was firmly in the government's lap.

It was in these circumstances that as Minister of State at the Board of Trade I was asked by Anthony Crosland, President of the Board of Trade, to undertake an enquiry into 'the structure of the textile industry'. The main question, though not the only question, was the Courtaulds bid for English Calico. The fact that the problem was presented to me in such general terms enabled me to consider other problems than just the Courtaulds bid. I was assisted in their personal capacities by Sir Joseph Lockwood, Chairman of IRC, and Sir James Steel, Chairman of the Textile Council. The enquiry was to be undertaken in the light of a report by the Textile Council on the productivity and efficiency of the textile industry which was about to be published and which was already in the hands of the Board of Trade. It was Douglas Jay who, as President of the Board of Trade (1964-67), had invited the Textile Council to make this report. We will later discuss its recommendation that there should be a new form of protection for the industry from Commonwealth imports, by tariff rather than by quota. Here we are concerned with its view that many firms would have to go out of existence, that employment in the industry would have to be heavily reduced, and that probably in the end there would be four or five major firms in the industry. These recommendations concerning the future structure and size of the industry were consistent with the view that further restructuring would be required, though not necessarily by Courtaulds.

One interpretation of my task was that what I had to do was produce a peace treaty between ICI and Courtaulds. The two battling giants were to lie down together and browse in accordance with rules to be drafted by me. But first, the principal impediment in the way of such peaceful behaviour would have to be removed, the impediment that was presented by Courtaulds' 'link' with its textile subsidiaries and the inhibition that link imposed on the free marketing of synthetic fibres. A proposal was presented to me which would achieve this purpose. It was the idea of a British Fibres Corporation. Under this proposal ICI would acquire Courtaulds' fibre production and establish a British Fibres Corporation as a wholly owned subsidiary. This would resolve the problem of the fibre textile link. With Courtaulds no longer involved in fibre production, that would eliminate one reason for preventing their takeover of English Calico. A variant of this proposal was to establish a British Fibres Corporation as a joint subsidiary of ICI and Courtaulds. This was less attractive because of the unhappy history of the ICI–Courtaulds partnership in British Nylon Spinners, a partnership which had been broken not so long before. Another variant of this proposal was a complete ICI takeover of Courtaulds. But this never seemed a runner.

The idea of a British Fibres Corporation in the first of the above forms had much support. It was at once dramatic and simple. It would solve the problem of the link and unleash Courtaulds unimpeded by *arrières pensées*, to rationalise the textile industry. The chairman of one major company—a strong supporter of the idea—offered to investigate on my behalf whether the proposal was feasible. I told him that he might indeed explore the ground but he must understand that I was not committed to the idea.

I was in fact a great deal less attracted to the idea than many of those in industry and elsewhere who were advising me. First I did not see that there was any public advantage to be derived from freeing ICI from Courtaulds' competition in fibres. But in any case I did not believe that it could be brought about by voluntary agreement. There would be, for example, great difficulty in valuing Courtaulds' cellulosic fibre assets, particularly if they were separated from Courtaulds' textile interests. This view was confirmed when my unofficial emissary returned to confess failure. In short, to achieve a British Fibres Corporation would involve the government in bringing powerful pressure to bear on both ICI and Courtaulds, and I did not believe that the arguments in favour of such a Corporation were anything like strong enough to justify this.

My own approach to the problem began with the presumption that competition should be encouraged, not discouraged, both among fibre manufacturers and within the textile industry. This principle suggested both that ICI should not take over Courtaulds' fibre production and that Courtaulds should not take over English Calico. There are, no doubt, situations, particularly in a market the size of the United Kingdom, in which it is right to accept a reduction in competition for the sake of other benefits, for example in productivity, that it may not otherwise be possible to obtain. There must, however, be strong reasons to think that these compensating benefits will actually accrue. The arguments, already summarised, which Courtaulds presented in support of their bid had therefore to be carefully assessed. There was also one other argument in favour of the bid which had to be set against my presumption in favour of competition. English Calico was known to be facing serious problems with the CPA part of its assets. There was questioning whether it had the management capacity to resolve those problems. However the fact that English Calico had serious problems did not mean that Courtaulds should be given the opportunity of solving them. Courtaulds had its own problems following its many takeovers of recent years. It might well be possible for the management of English Calico, a much smaller company, to do a better job itself than Courtaulds could do for it. At any rate it seemed to me that the risk was worth taking.

There was here a general problem. The five large textile companies had been built up very rapidly by a series of mergers. It was not at all clear that they had yet actually won the productivity and other gains that had been foreseen from those mergers. The Textile Council report itself encouraged these doubts by what it said on the subject. During the course of the enquiry I saw a number of leading retailers with close contact with the textile industry. They were not impressed by the integration so far achieved. The chairman of one of these retail companies spoke disparagingly of one of the British Big Five which had gained a particular reputation for the speed with which its mergers had been integrated. No doubt with some pardonable exaggeration, he said that whereas in buying from a German textile company he dealt with two men, a production director and a sales director, with this British company it seemed to be almost impossible to find a room large enough to accommodate all the people who had to be present at any deal.

I therefore decided to recommend a standstill on mergers between the five major companies in the textile industry. The standstill was to be temporary, although for an unstated period. Meanwhile it would not prevent minor acquisitions nor exchanges of surplus capacity between the Big Five. It could be argued that to protect any of the Big Five from the threat of takeover might remove pressure and thus slow rather than hasten their integration processes. The answer to that fear was twofold. First, competition in the textile industry should encourage these companies to realise their potential more fully. Secondly, they were not absolutely protected from takeovers. One day the standstill would end and by that time if not before they would have to be ready to prove their worth. In any case the standstill only applied to mergers among the Big Five. It would not prevent a bid from a company outside the industry. If such a bid occurred it would have to be considered by the Board of Trade under its normal merger powers.

As a result of the Monopolies Commission's report, the Board of Trade had power to ban further acquisitions by Courtaulds. That apart, there was no legal basis for the standstill. All the government could have done would have been to refer to the Monopolies Commission any proposed merger that contravened the standstill. The Monopolies Commission would then have been entitled to come to its own view of the merits of the particular merger before it. Thus, Courtaulds apart, the standstill was in fact no more than notice given by the government that it would refer to the Monopolies Commission mergers that contravened it. But that sufficed.

There remained the question of the 'link' on which ICI particularly pressed the government to take a decision. I could hardly take a position in favour of the link. I could not say that it was the government's view that fibre manufacturers should integrate forward into the textile industry, if fibre manufacturers' judgment of their own commercial interests was that they should not integrate forward. There were many arguments that moved me to think that in the United Kingdom situation, there were sound reasons for following, within sensible limits, the Courtaulds policy rather than the pure American principle of separation. But I did not see any merit at all in the government exerting even such pressure as an expression of view might have implied, on companies which saw their own interests differently.

In any case ICI was not asking me to declare in favour of the link but to declare against it. There was one very strong argument against the link, the argument that presumably had moved the Americans against it, the argument of competition policy. This type of verticalisation definitely did inhibit competition. As such this was an argument that appealed to me. But I had to base my view on the practical situation. The size of the United Kingdom market did prevent as generous a deployment of competitive forces as was possible in the USA. If I took the competition principle to its logical conclusion, I must recommend that Courtaulds be broken up. Even the Monopolies Commission had not proposed that.

Courtaulds could be stopped and was, by the standstill, being stopped from further major acquisitions for the time being at least. Therefore in practice a ban on the link would have no further immediate effect on Courtaulds than was in any case being achieved by the standstill. The practical effect of such a ban would simply be to prevent ICI from integrating forward. Although I did not foresee how rapidly ICI's attitude would change, I did think that there was not in principle so great a difference between Courtaulds' acquisition policy and ICI's financing policy, and that therefore one could not be sure that ICI's view of the link would stand unchanged for ever. It therefore seemed to me that a ban on the link, particularly in the circumstances of the standstill, would be against ICI's own interests.

It was true of course that the standstill was temporary and that therefore future acquisitions by Courtaulds were not ruled out. I felt this was a problem that could be confronted when we had to. Meanwhile ICI should be encouraged to think again about its policy in the actual practical United Kingdom situation, not inhibited from doing so. ICI was the only intimate participant in the struggle left virtually free of any control as to its future actions. As it was not one of the Big Five, the standstill did not apply to it. The government was of course free to consider any bid it made for any of the Big Five in the ordinary way, but ICI were not told in advance, as the others in fact were, that the government would oppose such a bid. The proposal that ICI, six months later, did make, to take over and merge *two* of the Big Five, was, of course, contrary to the standstill but only in that respect.

A ban on the link might have had one further effect. Courtaulds was planning to begin manufacture of polyester fibre. A ban might therefore be taken to imply that, even if the company was not broken up, it should not develop further synthetic fibre manufacture. I could see no argument for freeing ICI from such further competition in polyester fibres as Courtaulds might provide.

I therefore drafted the following sentences for a statement by the President of the Board of Trade:

Apart from the special difficulties arising from monopoly, the government do not consider that in the present circumstances they need to take a view of the linking of fibre production with textile manufacture. It follows that the government would see no objection if an existing fibre producer with textile interests wished to diversify into new fibres.

The reference in those sentences to 'special difficulties arising from monopoly' was a reference to the fact that there could be bids, for example by ICI, that would have serious monopoly implications and would have to be considered in that light.

As a matter of fact the government had no legal power to ban the link, though again it did have the power of reference to the Monopolies Commission. The decision to 'take no view' of the link was criticised by some commentators. The government had, they thought, missed an opportunity. They were apparently horrified at the idea of a government taking no view of something.

My recommendations, with which Lockwood and Steel were completely in accord, were accepted by the government. The government added one further decision. Courtaulds had claimed that their bid was intended to forestall an American bid. I was highly sceptical of the proposition that American companies were interested in takeovers of British textile companies. My temporary standstill proposal made no reference to foreign takeovers. It equally made no reference to takeovers by other British firms outside the textile industry. All such takeover bids could be considered on their merits if the occasion arose. The government, however, took the view that foreign takeovers of textile companies should be included in the standstill. I did not think this an important departure from my own proposal because I did not anticipate an American bid. The inclusion of foreign takeovers in the ban led, however, to Viyella claiming that the standstill had

D

prevented an arrangement between themselves and Burlington Mills.

It was this ban on foreign takeovers that secured the most unfavourable Press comment at the time. 'It is difficult to acquit the government of chauvinism', said *The Times* on 1 July 1969. Whatever the principle of the ban, the Press was led greatly to exaggerate the actual prospect of foreign takeovers of textile companies at that time.

English Calico, understandably, regarded Anthony Crosland's statement on 30 June 1969 announcing the standstill, as 'a wise decision'. Courtaulds described it as 'a useful clarification of the issues and quite acceptable to us'.

ICI welcomed the standstill and the fact that English Calico would retain independence and freedom to develop its own business. Its statement, however, added: 'We regret that the Government has not considered it necessary to take a view on the linking of fibre production with textile manufacture as in our view this aspect is as important to the freedom and prosperity of the textile industry.' [28]

Six months later ICI made its bid for Viyella and Carrington & Dewhurst. ICI was proposing, subject to government permission, to forge its own link. By this time the Ministry of Technology had taken over sponsorship of the textile industry. Another Committee under Harold Lever went over the ground again. The same idea of a British Fibres Corporation was once more floated, apparently from sources which had been disappointed by my lack of enthusiasm for the idea. Once more it sank without trace. But ICI was permitted to go ahead with its takeover on conditions regarding its equity holding in the merged company. There was also to be a code of conduct for fibre producers. These conditions were evidently considered necessary because ICI wanted Viyella as well as Carrington & Dewhurst. They represented an interesting paradox. They seemed to imply that in the view of the government the link was undesirable at a time when any idea of banning the link was being finally abandoned as an inevitable result of the consent given to the double takeover.

[28] *Daily Telegraph* 1 July 1969

Neither condition has in fact proved practicable. ICI retains its equity holding.[29] The code of conduct was never written.

It was stated that the standstill was to continue in the new situation created by the ICI takeover. There have in fact been no further mergers between the Big Five, now the Big Four, in the textile industry, though presumably the standstill is no longer government policy.

There are strong arguments against forms of enquiry such as were undertaken, first by myself, and later by Harold Lever, into the structure of the textile industry. Although highly publicised, they are in fact secret. The conclusions are announced but neither reasons for those conclusions nor the evidence have to be exposed in the sort of detail which the Monopolies Commission considers appropriate in its reports. The public has to be satisfied with such indication of reasoning as may be provided in a statement or in a Press briefing. There is more than a hint of the smoke-filled room about it all. As a result, the affairs of citizens are disposed of in a manner which affords them no appeal and perhaps not even the satisfaction of knowing why the decision has gone against them. As in this case, decisions may be taken at brief intervals which are not entirely consistent. Such enquiries, however fairly conducted, are therefore not in accordance with the highest principles of the rule of law. Any citizen who feels aggrieved by the decisions of such enquiries is, therefore, entitled to his grievance, the more so as he has no remedy.

There are however many matters, not just involving mergers, that arise in the relations between government and industry that require to be determined politically. The history here recounted could be regarded as the history of a conflict of principles, competition versus restructuring, vertical integration versus freedom in the selection of suppliers. More realistically it was a clash between two great powers. The government had looked on with acceptance, and indeed approval, while Courtaulds restructured the textile industry. ICI then said that a particular merger would be against its

---

[29] ICI has undertaken to use only such voting power as it would have if its holding had been reduced to 35 per cent.

interests and it said it in such a way that the government was forced to listen. One object of policy is to seek to convert political situations into situations which can be resolved in the full light of day in accordance with known rules. That is obviously the course of fairness and openness. It is an ideal, but an ideal that cannot always rule in political situations. At the time, the government was confronted with a political situation and political situations do tend to get resolved in smoke-filled rooms. Power remains a fact of life and another object of policy is to resolve peacefully confrontations between the powerful and to do it, preferably, in ways that do no harm, or the least possible harm, to those lacking the divisions which would entitle them to a seat at the table. Governments have a special responsibility to speak at the table for the otherwise unrepresented. It would be difficult to claim that the unrepresented suffered from the decisions taken by either the Dell or the Lever enquiries, and that at least was a small mercy.

Chapter 4

THE NATION STATE
AS A PROTECTIVE DEVICE

1. *Introduction*

Major decisions in industrial policy often involve relations with other countries. This chapter illustrates the working of industrial policy in its international context.

In Chapter 2, the nation state was described as inevitably a protective device. Human conflict consists not just of physical violence, or what Hobbes called the 'disposition thereto'. It appears also in competition for worldly goods. There have in the past been wars for trade as well as for empire. Empires indeed have been conquered not just by emperors in search of power but by merchants in search of trade. More recently, governments have sought to agree civilised rules in accordance with which countries may peacefully compete for trade to the general benefit as well as to that of their own nation.

There are here two different processes at work. In one, nations co-operate for the general good. They fix exchange rates, they lower tariffs, they create common markets. They hope thereby to maximise international trade, the opportunity for economic growth and for their own nation to benefit from the forward thrust of the international community. But at the same time as they are co-operating to create an ambience favourable to economic growth, they are each of them striving to strengthen their own hand in the competition for a share in that growth. The fact therefore that nations conclude treaties to govern rules of conduct, does not mean that trade does not have something of the character of war.

In such a war national governments cannot simply remain

as benevolent spectators of their peoples' efforts. They cannot leave everything to the unregulated impact of international free trade on their domestic economies with, at best, temporary 'safeguard' procedures available to help adjust a declining industry to the new competitive situation. It is for this reason that when one set of supports for national industry, such as the tariff, is negotiated away in whole or in part, other types of support begin to creep in under the name of industrial policy. To promote the most rapid expansion of international trade, governments have been expected to surrender some sovereignty in relation to their own national economies. But there is an irrevocable sovereignty which compels a government to act in support of its people when it believes they need support. The people of any country have the right to regard their government as their own, primarily responsible to them, and only very much secondarily to any international community.

When a government enters into international agreements to reduce trade barriers, it does so because it sees this as the best way of discharging its responsibility to its people. When it takes back something of what it has conceded, it does so because it believes that the actual working of the agreements has been in some respect unfavourable to its people. There is a balance of advantage and disadvantage which governments try to hold. In holding that balance, they have to remember the possibility of retaliation against any excess of protectionism. Different countries are exposed to different extents to that threat.

In this chapter three examples are given of the way in which UK governments have operated protective policies over the last few years. The first is an account of the UK's relations with EFTA. It shows how international pressures can operate and how governments sometimes feel themselves compelled to concede something to those pressures. It includes a summary of the international aspects of the aluminium smelter project. The second is an account of the way that project was managed. The story of the aluminium smelter project illustrates many facets of the actual working of industrial policy against a background of balance of payments deficit. A point which will be taken up later is how international criticism can represent a far more difficult hurdle than in this country is parliamentary control or criticism. The third example deals with the changing relationship between the UK government and multinational companies. In the past, this relationship has been almost pure *laissez-faire*. Recently the UK government, as have other governments, has become rather more determined to ensure by calculated action that the operations of multinational companies do benefit the UK economy. There is less willingness to leave this to the chance of market forces. The exploitation of North Sea oil is providing UK governments with an opportunity to rethink their relationship with multinational companies.

2. *Britain and the European Free Trade Area*

EFTA was founded in 1960 to promote free trade in manufactured goods between Austria, Denmark, Norway, Portugal, Sweden, Switzerland and the UK. The seven members had a total population of about one hundred million. Half of this population was provided by just one member, the United Kingdom. Thus for the other six countries, free access to the United Kingdom market for their manufactured goods was the principal advantage to be expected from the EFTA Convention. Everything done by the United Kingdom government to protect the British market or to build up its national industry was seen by the other EFTA countries as a breach of the Convention or at least, depriving them of benefits they had expected from their membership of EFTA.

Early in the life of EFTA, on 15 October 1964, a Labour Government with interventionist inclinations was elected in the United Kingdom. It found a large deficit in the country's balance of payments. Yet for reasons which then seemed good to it, it did not wish to devalue. Instead it introduced a 15 per cent import surcharge on manufactured imports from any source. Although the surcharge left the other EFTA countries with exactly the same preference over the other foreign exporters to the United Kingdom market as they had before, it placed them at a disadvantage as compared with British manufacturers in the British market. The result was strong pressure for the removal of the surcharge. There was the possibility of retaliation. Such was the pressure that hardly a month after introducing the surcharge, the British government had conceded in principle the idea of an early reduction. At the end of April 1965 the surcharge was reduced to 10 per cent. In November 1966 it was removed altogether, thus speeding the inevitable slide to devaluation. When in 1968, after devaluation, the balance of payments was seen not to be responding as rapidly as had been hoped, the British government introduced an import deposit scheme. The reaction of the other EFTA countries was somewhat more tolerant than it had been in 1964 and 1965. In any case by this time the British government was clearer on its priorities. Its responsibilities to its own people came first.

The instincts of a country cursed with slow economic growth and a perennial balance of payments problem are likely to turn towards protectionism. Protection can be provided not merely by tariff barriers but by government intervention of various kinds in support of national industry. Thus it was not surprising that the inclinations of the Labour Government of 1964-70 should be interventionist. The Industrial Reorganisation Corporation was established to promote mergers that might be of benefit to the national economy. The section on the IRC in Chapter 3 has explained why its activities in promoting mergers could be seen as just another protective device comparable with such other protective devices as import surcharges and deposits.

One merger was in the ball-bearing industry and it was consummated by the IRC in a way which brought together the British-owned elements in that industry at the expense of the Swedish ball-bearing company, SKF, which was planning a takeover of a British ball-bearing company. Thus in this case, to the fundamental fear of the protectionist implications of IRC-type action in general there was added, in Sweden's view, a challenge to the right of establishment guaranteed by Article 16 of the EFTA Convention which required that there should be no discrimination in the United Kingdom against firms of foreign EFTA origin any more than there should be in other EFTA countries against firms of United Kingdom origin. The Swedish Ambassador was instructed to make representations to the British government against the activities of the IRC in this case. The British government received the representations but, naturally, did no more than note them.

Other cases were more difficult to handle. A low rate of investment has frequently been diagnosed as a cause of Britain's low rate of economic growth. The Labour Government therefore sought a form of investment incentive more effective than the tax allowances offered by previous Conservative governments. The answer was found in the investments grant system. There was in addition the problem of the development areas which were lagging particularly seriously in industrial development. Therefore, whereas in the country as a whole the rate of investment grant was 20 per cent, in the development areas it was 40 per cent. The object was to strengthen British manufacturing industry. Because of that very fact the system was opprobrious to our EFTA partners. They regarded it as a straight subsidy.

No British government could fail to take the action it felt necessary in British development areas simply because of EFTA objections. The investment grants system therefore went ahead despite EFTA criticism that it violated the rules of competition and in particular Article 13 of the Convention on 'Government Aids' which said, among other things, that member states should not maintain or introduce any form of aid the main purpose or effect of which is to frustrate the benefits expected from the removal or absence of duties and quantitative restrictions on trade between member states.

It was the aluminium smelter project that brought Britain's relations with EFTA to their lowest ebb. Large-scale aluminium smelting in Britain was made possible by a combination of investment grants at the development area rate with electricity supplied not at ordinary grid prices, but at a much lower price related to the cost of production at an advanced gas-cooled nuclear reactor. The Labour Government's interest in the project arose principally from the expected import saving, about £15 million sterling per annum for every 100,000 tons of aluminium smelted in Britain. Politically it had the further advantage of corresponding to the bright technological image which the Labour Government wished to create. The EFTA country directly affected was Norway which was at the time Britain's principal supplier of unwrought aluminium, having recently overtaken Canada in that role, owing to the commercial decisions of Alcan which smelted in Norway as well as in Canada. Norway claimed that the aluminium smelter project in Britain frustrated a benefit she had had every reason to expect from the EFTA Convention. It breached the sensible division of labour with EFTA. Norway, with its cheap hydro-electric power, was the obvious economic source of aluminium for EFTA countries. It was difficult for Norway to protest against the pricing of the electricity for the British project. There is in principle nothing wrong with pricing electricity for specific purposes at prices related to the cost of production at particular generating plants rather than at average grid prices. Norway did it herself. So did many other countries.

The point of attack therefore was the investment grant system. No nuclear reactor could supply electricity at prices comparable with hydro-electricity in Norway. The electricity therefore would not have been cheap enough to make aluminium smelting economic had it not been for the subsidy on the plant represented by the 40 per cent investment grant. Moreover in pointing the attack on the investment grant system, Norway rallied the other EFTA countries against Britain. The aluminium smelter project was, Norway argued, only one example of the way in which the subsidy to investment provided by the investment grant system could distort competition within EFTA to the advantage of Britain and to the disadvantage of the other EFTA countries.

Governments cannot simply ignore such pressure from their trading partners. One way of meeting it is to persuade one's partners that one's actions are not inconsistent with international commitments. Britain did have a case. The aluminium smelter project did not frustrate any benefit that Norway had a right to expect from EFTA. Import of aluminium into Britain was free of tariff from any source (except Eastern Europe), not just from EFTA sources. The supply of aluminium throughout the free world was controlled by a handful of major aluminium producers, three of whom were involved in the three separate smelters proposed for Britain. There was no compulsion at all on Alcan to continue to supply Britain from Norway as it had recently been doing if, for example, it found it convenient to revert to supplying Britain from Canada. It could, if it wished, find other outlets than Britain for its Norwegian aluminium. Obviously if it ceased to supply Britain from Norway it would find other outlets for its Norwegian aluminium if only because of its large investment in Norwegian aluminium as a result of which it had a Norwegian government director on its main board. If Britain denied Alcan, or other producers, the right to smelt in Britain this by no means meant that Norway would benefit. Aluminium smelted at a smelter erected, for example, at Bantry Bay in Eire supplied with electricity generated from cheap oil carried in vast tankers and sub- sidised liberally by the Irish government, would gain free entry into Britain just as much as would aluminium from any EFTA source. Therefore for Britain to decide not to go ahead would not necessarily benefit EFTA. It would certainly damage the United Kingdom.

Actually it was expected that it would be Canada, not Norway, that suffered principally from the smelting of aluminium in Britain. Supply from British Aluminium's new smelter at Invergordon in Scotland was to replace supply from a smelter in Canada which British Aluminium proposed to sell. The British government had, perhaps, less sensitivity about the aluminium trade with Canada than about that with Norway in view of Canada's overwhelmingly favourable trade balance with the United Kingdom. The parallel row with Canada served to confirm, in Britain's view, that this was not an EFTA matter but a matter related to Britain's international trade in general, that Norway had no special status in the question arising out of her membership of EFTA. Norway had no more complaint against Britain than Britain had against Norway about motor cars. Just as the import of unwrought aluminium into Britain was free of tariff from all sources, not just from EFTA countries, so was the import of cars into Norway. Just as British membership of EFTA brought us no advantage over Germany in the supply of motor cars to Norway, Norway could expect no extra advantage in the supply of aluminium to Britain.

Basically the logic of Britain's argument was that Britain must do those things that were seen to be in its national interest and that as a matter of fact what was being done in this case was not inconsistent with any international obligation. The real question was whether Britain could get away with it or whether the weight of international pressure would prove too much.

In fact Britain decided to concede two points. It reduced the initial projected capacity from 300,000 tons to 260,000 tons by reducing the Anglesey and Invergordon plants from 120,000 tons to 100,000 tons each. And it offered to review any further expansion of the project with EFTA in the light of the actual impact on Norway's trade. Thus probably for the first time in British history, a British government promised to consult foreign governments about the expansion of a British industry. With those two concessions, Britain decided to go ahead with the aluminium smelter project over Norway's protests. Norway could have taken the question officially through the EFTA complaints procedure. Had the complaint been upheld, Norway would have been entitled to retaliate against Britain's trade. But to take such a course against the dominant partner in EFTA would have put at risk the support of the other EFTA countries. Norway decided, though grumbling, to desist.

This is not perhaps the most glorious episode in Britain's history. Countries driven into protectionist attitudes do not appear at their best any more than do countries driven into devaluation. Countries in persistent deficit are more likely to adopt protectionist or autarchic attitudes than they would in a world in which it was made easier to achieve balance of payments equilibrium at a higher rather than a lower level. Where international trade is war, countries will protect themselves. When they protect themselves it will sometimes happen that smaller countries, entirely innocent of any economic aggression, may suffer. Thus President Nixon's measures of 15 August 1971 did not discriminate in favour of Britain despite the USA's long-standing trading surplus with the United Kingdom.

Where there is better international co-operation, countries can be more open in their attitudes to foreign trade. They will have a greater incentive to benefit from the international division of labour if they know that it will not simply be an instrument whereby some countries build up large and persistent surpluses at the expense of others. In such a world there might not have been a British aluminium smelter project, although it is fair to say that it would have had to be a rather perfect world, with strong guarantees against aggression, because otherwise there would be continuing uncertainty as to when economic aggression might break out again. The international trading and monetary systems must find some way of reconciling the protection of national interests with the expansion of international trade. A government's constituency is its nation, not the world. That will continue to be the case, for Britain as for other member countries, even in EEC.

3. *The Aluminium Smelter Project*
It is convenient at this point to continue the discussion of the Aluminium Smelter decision in a slightly different context. Its purpose is to illustrate how the impact of the external environment—in this case as exemplified by a chronic balance of payments deficit—can call forth industrial responses attractive to a government determined not to seek the more natural solution of exchange rate adjustment. Not all acts of industrial policy originate from the government; but inevitably it is the government that has to respond, decide and take responsibility.

During 1966 a paper was prepared in the offices of RTZ in London. It pointed out that with the benefit of electricity at a price related to the cost of production at an Advanced Gas Cooled Reactor, and with investment grants on plant and machinery at the development area rate of 40 per cent, it would be possible to smelt aluminium economically in Britain. The cost of the electricity from an AGR would not be comparable with hydro-electricity. But investment grants at 40 per cent on the plant and machinery in the smelter and the reactor might close the gap. Investment grants, unlike investment allowances, act directly to reduce the capital cost of plant and machinery. It therefore becomes easier to make a profit on a project.

The RTZ paper was not produced for academic reasons. RTZ had discovered bauxite in Australia. They thus needed to find outlets for this raw material. Bauxite is the raw material at the beginning of the process that leads through alumina to the smelting of aluminium. A large aluminium smelter in the United Kingdom could be part of RTZ's answer.

A proposal was therefore made to the government through the Board of Trade. A large smelter (possibly of 240,000 tons) would be built in the United Kingdom. It would be built in a development area to obtain the benefit of the 40 per cent rate of investment grant. As RTZ did not possess aluminium smelting knowhow, the smelter would be built in collaboration with Kaiser, one of the great American aluminium companies. Outlets would be needed for the aluminium when smelted. RTZ was not at the time a supplier of aluminium in the United Kingdom. BICC, the cable manufacturers, who are large consumers of aluminium, would therefore be associated with the project and help to provide a market. The electricity would be generated at an AGR. As RTZ had no experience of the construction of a nuclear power plant, this would be built in collaboration with the Atomic Energy Authority. The large surplus of electricity beyond what was required for the smelter would be sold to the Grid. Both smelter and AGR were to benefit from the 40 per cent investment grant.

This was perhaps the most ingenious proposal ever put to government by a firm in the private sector. It had great attractions. There would be significant import savings. A new technological industry would be created in the United

Kingdom based on the use of nuclear energy in which the United Kingdom was a pioneer. The project would also provide some employment in a development area, particularly during construction, but also permanently thereafter.

Government economists calculated that an import saving of the expected size justified the resources that would be consumed. From the government's point of view there were, however, difficulties. It was unlikely that RTZ, even with the help of BICC and Kaiser, would be able to dispose of such a large quantity of aluminium, since they were involved only to a small extent in its subsequent fabrication. It is normal in the aluminium industry for the major companies to be engaged in both smelting and fabrication and the principal UK fabricators, British Aluminium and Alcan, obtained their metal from their own smelters in Canada and Norway. There was after all no tariff on the import of unwrought aluminium into the United Kingdom. Then there was a series of problems associated with the power station. Was it right to permit the private ownership of a vast nuclear power station? AGRs are most efficient in very large sizes. The output would be far beyond what would be required for the smelter. There were particular problems concerned with the fact that this would be a partly privately owned nuclear station. There were other problems associated with the idea of giving a 40 per cent investment grant on this power station. The Central Electricity Generating Board did not receive investment grants. Other private power stations did not get them. One could hardly allow the grant to this AGR but deny it to other generators of electricity, whether in the public or private sector. At the very least this would open up the possibility of a vast increase in public expenditure, most of it for no discernible national benefit. The government therefore concluded that the grant would have to be limited to the smelter and could not be made available on the AGR.

For these reasons the government turned down the RTZ proposal, and began to consider whether there was any other way of achieving the same object. At the time the government was criticised for this decision. Yet there was an additional, quite conclusive, argument against the RTZ proposal, an argument just as conclusive for RTZ as for the government, though at this stage in the negotiation it was an unspoken argument. *Nobody had yet built a full-scale AGR.* Indeed, as late as 1972 not a single AGR had yet been completed, although the first AGR, Dungeness B, was ordered in 1966 and although four other AGRs were also under construction. The technical risks, the risks of cost escalation, were enormous. They were particularly large on early AGRs. Such risks could gravely imperil a private company, even one as large as RTZ. Thus although the RTZ objective was acceptable to the government, the RTZ method was not and, indeed, on further consideration would not have been to RTZ either.

The ball was therefore in the government's court to decide whether there was any other way of establishing aluminium smelting in the United Kingdom. The steps in the answer were in principle quite simple. Investment grants would be made available on the cost of plant and machinery in the smelter as for any other industrial investment in a development area. The price of the electricity would be related to the cost of generating it in an AGR belonging to a nationalised Generating Board. But how could one justify charging the smelter a much lower price for electricity (that is a price related to the most modern type of nuclear generating plant) than was charged to the rest of industry whose prices were related to the average cost of production over the whole Grid? The answer to that question was found in the so-called Special Electricity Contract. It was decided that where there was a large new demand for electricity or, possibly, where an existing large demand might otherwise be lost, the government would consider authorising a Generating Board to offer consumers or potential consumers a Special Electricity Contract. Under a Special Electricity Contract, the purchaser of electricity would enter into a two-part agreement with a Generating Board. First he would pay to the Generating Board a sum related to the capital cost of a tranche of a specified AGR sufficient for his electricity requirements. Thus if, for example, the electricity requirement was 150 mW., the purchaser of the electricity would pay to the Generating Board the capital cost of a tranche of the AGR sufficient to produce 150 mW. The purchaser would not own the tranche but would command the electricity output from it. Under the second part of the agreement, the purchaser, having paid the capital cost of the tranche, would enter into an agreement for the payment of its share of the running costs of the AGR. In an AGR, capital cost is large relative to running cost. Thus the purchaser, after paying the final cost of the tranche, was to a significant extent guaranteed against inflation of his electricity costs.

The concept of the Special Electricity Contract was fine. But did it serve the purpose? The purpose of having a Special Electricity Contract would be achieved only if under it electricity could be supplied at a price that would make possible the smelting of aluminium in the United Kingdom. The essential difference between the Special Electricity Contract and the original RTZ scheme, apart from the question of ownership of the AGR, was that whereas under the RTZ scheme there would have been a 40 per cent investment grant on the AGR, under the Special Electricity Contract there was not because the nationalised Generating Boards were not eligible to receive investment grants on their power stations. Would therefore the Special Electricity Contract result in a cheap enough price for the electricity?

The government had no independent knowledge of what electricity prices were necessary. It had no technical knowledge of its own on aluminium smelting. That knowledge is in theory widely available in textbooks. In practice the knowhow is limited to companies smelting aluminium, in particular to the small number of large aluminium companies that dominate the world supply of aluminium. There was only one method of finding out what was the highest price an aluminium smelter could pay for its electricity. That method was to get a number of aluminium companies to compete for a Special Electricity Contract, that is to offer in competition the highest price that a smelter built by that company could pay for electricity. If that price was within the range of prices that might be produced from a Special Electricity Contract, a deal could be done. Otherwise, not. The incentive for the aluminium companies was the opportunity a successful tender would create for them, of smelting aluminium within the UK.

An announcement was therefore made, initially at the Labour Party Conference in September 1967, inviting tenders for Special Electricity Contracts in respect of one smelter of 120,000 tons capacity for completion in 1971 and another smelter of 120,000 tons capacity for completion in 1974. Tenders were to be examined by the Industrial Re-organisation Corporation which would make recommendations to the government. In order to conciliate Lord Robens, the Chairman of the National Coal Board, it was also stated that proposals based on coal could be made. By this time both the traditional suppliers of aluminium to the United Kingdom market, Alcan and British Aluminium, had been alerted to the threat to their positions, had realised the opportunity that was being created and were interested in the idea of constructing smelters of their own in the United Kingdom. It was known that Alcan might be interested in a smelter powered by a generating plant of its own fuelled by coal. Alcan had experience elsewhere in the world of coal-fuelled electricity generation for smelters. A Special Electricity Contract was, in any case, less suitable for Alcan as they proposed in the first place to erect only 60,000 tons of capacity though they did intend to expand to 120,000 tons later. The coal option was therefore likely to be of more interest to Alcan than to the other contenders.

The contenders located sites for smelters. The sites had to be in development areas to benefit from the 40 per cent grant. But preferably they had also to be in deep-water ports to permit entry of the large bulk carriers bringing alumina, the raw material for the smelters. RTZ had a site at Anglesey. British Aluminium and Alcan each had sites in mind at Invergordon on the Moray Firth. If there was to be only one smelter by 1971, England would in any case be left out. It would be Scotland or Wales. One or other of the smaller nations of Great Britain would be jealous and angry.

In fact, three tenders came in, from the RTZ Consortium, from British Aluminium and from Alcan. The IRC made its recommendations to the government. It placed the tenders in order of merit but argued that there was no reason why the government should not in fact authorise two smelters rather than one for completion by 1971. While the details of the IRC recommendations were not made public, it was clear that their preference would be for RTZ and British Aluminium. As Alcan intended to start with only 60,000 tons of capacity, the balance of payments saving from their smelter would in the earlier years be smaller than that from the proposed 120,000 ton smelters of RTZ and British Aluminium.

Meanwhile on 18 November 1967 the pound was devalued. This devaluation increased the import price of aluminium in sterling terms. That fact in its turn made possible an increase in the price that a United Kingdom smelter could economically pay for its electricity.

The way the aluminium smelter project was developing was totally unsatisfactory to Alcan, one of the two principal traditional suppliers of aluminium to the United Kingdom market. From Alcan's point of view the project was taking on the appearance of a conspiracy by RTZ, aided and abetted by the British government, to deprive Alcan of a valuable market. Alcan therefore decided to fight. They initiated propaganda in Scotland in favour of their project at Invergordon, propaganda that by clear implication was hostile to the British government. But their master stroke was to enter into a contract with the National Coal Board for the supply of coal from a pit at Lynemouth to their proposed smelter at Invergordon. Thus they gained the support of the miners' lobby. Moreover Lord Robens made clear publicly that he would only finalise the contract with Alcan if the government approved. The government was faced with the problem of either approving the contract or of outraging the miners. There was at the time some surprise that the NCB could supply coal at a sufficiently attractive price. The Central Electricity Generating Board was certainly surprised that the NCB had available such cheap coal and yet was not supplying it to them as the NCB's largest customer.

In fact the Alcan deal had certain advantages from the point of view of the government. The government had no dogmatic view that Alcan should be excluded. The coal contract was within the NCB's commercial discretion. Although Robens had asked for government approval, in fact, unlike with the Special Electricity Contract, no government authorisation for the deal was necessary. The deal was to that extent less sensitive internationally. If Alcan could be persuaded to locate its smelter at Lynemouth where the coal came from, it would round off rather prettily the conflict of competing nationalisms. There would be smelters each for England, Scotland and Wales. The fact that coal would be playing its part in the smelter project would please the miners and, after all, the additional smelter would add to the balance of payments saving. Internationally there was some benefit in having Alcan involved in view of their participation in aluminium smelting in Canada and Norway, the two countries from which our aluminium imports mainly came. Thus, in fact, Alcan was pushing at an open door.

Detailed negotiations with the three companies began in April 1968. In these negotiations there were many difficult problems to solve. Within the government a multi-disciplinary, inter-departmental, team of officials was set up with the author in the chair as chief negotiator on behalf of the government. Alcan was persuaded to go to Lynemouth. The Generating Boards concluded Special Electricity Contracts with British Aluminium and the RTZ Consortium. Loans were made under the Industrial Expansion Act to cover the capital contribution for the tranches of two AGRs which British Aluminium and the RTZ Consortium had to pay to the Generating Boards under the terms of the Special Electricity Contract. This money could not be borrowed in the market because, owing to the peculiar terms of the Special Electricity Contract, the tranche of the AGR did not become an asset of the contributing company. To borrow in the market, therefore, might prejudice the wider borrowing capacity of the parent companies. The government therefore agreed to lend this money.

The deal with Alcan, which did not involve a Special Electricity Contract, was the first to be concluded. Heads of agreement between the government and the other two companies on the one hand, and the Generating Boards and the two companies on the other, were concluded by the end of July 1968. The orders under the Industrial Expansion Act were approved by the House of Commons in November 1968. The first of the smelters, that at Anglesey, was officially opened on 25 June 1971 by the Secretary of State for Wales in a government which had just abolished investment grants.

A series of questions arises from this account of the Aluminium Smelter Project. The first is whether it was sensible for the British government to use public money to help private companies to smelt aluminium in the United Kingdom, a country lacking extensive cheap sources of hydro-electric power. This question takes on a new dimension in the light of present more flexible attitudes to exchange rate changes and the effect such attitudes have in easing a nation's task of balancing its payments with the rest of the world. The concept of import saving is by its nature protectionist. It may be that in a less protectionist climate than that of 1966-68 the government would have decided not to go ahead with the Aluminium Smelter Project. On the other hand, here was a project proposed to the government by a private company. Compared with the import saving available, it was not excessively costly. The loans are repayable The main cost to the government consisted of the investment grants. There were potential costs to the Generating Boards and the NCB, but the concept of the Special Electricity Contract was intended to ensure that the Generating Boards would be protected from loss, and other consumers from paying any more for their electricity than they would have done had these contracts not been entered into. The Generating Boards themselves were statutorily bound to protect both their own interests and those of their other customers. The NCB contract with Alcan had been freely entered into by the NCB on its own initiative. The cost to the government does not of course cover the whole resource cost to the nation. In theory the resources devoted to creating aluminium smelters could have been deployed elsewhere in activities more naturally competitive. There is no evidence however that alternative uses for these resources would in fact have come forward. Here was a specific proposal backed by private money and it would have been difficult for a government to turn it down just on *laissez-faire* principles, if a practical method of advancing it could be found.

What of the competence of the government machine in handling and negotiating a project once the principle was accepted? There were complaints at the time about delays. From first conception in the RTZ offices to final agreement, it took two years. Nevertheless much had had to be done during those two years. The RTZ proposal was highly original and of a kind certainly unprecedented in the relations between government and industry in the United Kingdom. The government had to consider the initial proposal. When it decided that it had to reject it in the form initially proposed, it had to work out an alternative proposal. There then had to be time for the companies to tender for the Special Electricity Contract, for the IRC to make their recommendations, and for the government to negotiate the very complex contracts. There is no doubt that the patience of the companies was sorely tried. It might however be found, on investigation, that the gestation period in industry of far less radical ideas is not invariably so much shorter than two years. Sir Val Duncan, Chairman of RTZ, told the Expenditure Committee in July 1971 (Q.1370): 'I think that the Board of Trade team did extremely well in these negotiations. . . . I think the Board of Trade team were very competent.' He did, however, suggest that there should have been a team of people whose whole time was devoted to this particular operation, rather than 'rushing from this to meetings on totally unrelated subjects day after day and week after week which must be very difficult.' It is undoubtedly true that a project of this complexity is likely to be better handled if there is continuity among those handling it. Nevertheless, despite everything so freely said about the Civil Service, including by the Fulton Committee, the Board of Trade proved to have the technical capacity to carry the negotiations through to success. This was not in any case a project that could have been handled by a para-governmental agency. It involved a political decision by the government, a decision which had international as well as domestic implications. It also involved what is sometimes called 'political will'. The mere decision by the government to go ahead did not in itself ensure successful completion of the negotiations. That decision was not rapturously received in all departments of government nor among every-one in the Generating Boards. Such obstacles were likely to be overcome only if the lead was taken by government itself.

The Aluminium Smelter Project was barely debated in Parliament at all. Questions were asked about it. Statements were made at various stages of the negotiations. But the only debates were one thirty-minute adjournment debate about the Alcan smelter and the two brief debates required under the Industrial Expansion Act before approval was given by the House of Commons to the two orders authorising the loans. On the Tory backbenches there was a small number of opponents of the project who based their arguments on *laissez-faire* principles and also on a claim that the project was inconsistent with the EFTA Convention. The attitude of the official Opposition was to condemn delay rather than to attack the principle. Politically the project was far too popular, particularly in Scotland and Wales, for it to be easy for the Conservative Party to attack it, however unhappy many of them may at the time have been about it. The Conservative Party was in fact in the ambiguous position of supporting a project made possible by investment grants while they were proposing to abolish investment grants should they return to office. The political pressure behind the project was reinforced by the Prime Minister's statement at the 1967 Labour Party Conference which would have made it a grave embarrassment had it proved impossible to reach agreement with the companies. The result was that the principle of the project was never properly discussed in Parliament. Much in the agreements—the price of the electricity, the value of the investment grants—was confidential. But sufficient informa-tion was available for a critical assessment if Parliament had wished to undertake it. In fact, the project has never been considered in any depth either by Parliament or by any Select Committee of Parliament. One could hardly claim that there was adequate, or indeed any significant, parliamentary control of government decisions in this field. Far greater control was exercised by our EFTA partners breathing down our necks and watching every move, than was exercised by Parliament in whom nominally the chief duty of oversight lay. Indeed, the evidence of this particular episode is that governments have to work much harder to justify their interventions in industry to their partners in international communities than they are ever likely to have to do to win the support of Parliament.

Was there anything else that could be learned from the smelter project? It was proposed when the negotiations had been completed that the participants, including the government, should sit down and consider in what respects the project could have been better handled. In fact, no such consideration was ever given. New preoccupations absorbed the energies of those involved. There is some reluctance to rake over one's mistakes when there is not much to be gained from so doing. There was a fairly general conviction that in this case very little was to be gained. The companies were not likely to be involved again in a project of this character with the United Kingdom government. Nor was there any comparable proposal from any other source before the government. Another product where the price of the electricity was known to be critical was chlorine. If the chlorine producers had put up a proposal for a Special Electricity Contract, and the government had decided to authorise it, no doubt an attempt would have been made to deploy the same team of people to handle the negotiation. But no such proposal in fact emerged during the lifetime of the Labour Government. The Aluminium Smelter Project proved to be 'one off'. It no doubt added to the store of experience of each one of the participants. There was no body of doctrine to be derived from so exceptional an episode.

There was perhaps just one commercial lesson to be learned. The government had been a little insouciant in not foreseeing the strength of the Alcan reaction to what with some reason appeared at one stage as being an attack on their market. It is as well, if governments involve themselves in activities which so drastically change the competitive position and so greatly affect market shares, that they should at least first consider the implications in that respect of what they are doing. But in fact, in this case, the confrontation between the company and the government ended agreeably to both and nothing was lost by the government's failure to study that aspect of the question sufficiently in advance.

The aluminium smelters are the most original product of the Labour Government's industrial policies. But originality has not in this case tempted imitation.

4. *The State and the Multinational Company*

Fashions change, and whereas only a few years ago the activities of so-called multinational companies were thought of as bringing undoubted benefits to this country, today there is questioning. Those concerned with the formation of industrial policy have to take a view.

For many years some countries have attempted by means of various types of control to ensure that there will be a balance of advantage to them before permitting an inward investment. They evidently have not been prepared to leave matters entirely to chance. Now in this country too we have begun to ask whether we have correctly assessed the balance of advantage and disadvantage, and if it is right to leave it so much to chance to determine whether, in the United Kingdom, the balance is in fact favourable. Governments are being pressed to exert their responsibility. They have long attracted foreign enterprise by their incentives but are now being pressed to ensure that there is an adequate return on the incentive offered. They find themselves in a situation in which in order to protect national interests in international trade, they have to negotiate not just with other governments but with great international companies.

International or multinational companies are in fact national companies which invest abroad widely and on a large scale. They might be defined as national companies which are large enough and free enough to be able to take advantage of the policies of foreign governments competing for their investments. Unilever and Shell are Anglo-Dutch.

Most of these companies are American or British. That national companies of this kind should have been allowed to walk off with the name 'international' or 'multinational', even in official reports on the international monetary and trading system, is one of the most remarkable achievements of modern marketing. It is a success attributable in no small measure to IBM, a company which epitomises *le défi Américain*, and whose remarkable market dominance throughout the West in the computer industry has led it to camouflage somewhat this blunt aspect of American technological leadership.

Yet IBM is an American company. Though, following the example of the Roman Empire, it has allowed foreigners to achieve senior positions in the company, unlike the Roman Empire it has not yet allowed a foreigner to be Emperor. The idea that there is some international community to which international companies owe allegiance may be suggested by the name but is not supported by the facts. The name can be regarded as a successful marketing promotion which should probably be illegal under the Trade Descriptions Act.[1]

Inward investment into this country has been virtually free of control and has been actively sought. Exchange control permission for a foreign takeover has never been refused. British governments have normally preferred inward investors to invest in new projects rather than to take over British firms. Successive governments did go so far as to impose conditions on Ford of America when it took over the independent capital invested in Ford UK, on Chrysler when it took over Rootes and on Philips when it took over Pye. But such takeovers have never been prohibited. The only examples of a government indicating that a foreign takeover would not be permitted have been in the cases of ICL, the national computer company, and, following the Textile Structure Enquiry, the big five textile companies protected under the

---

[1] The British are entitled to resent the fact that Disraeli, who was one of our earliest marketing men and who called the British Empire into existence in order to redress the balance between social classes in Britain, did not have the idea of calling it the International Empire. This failure of imagination probably shortened its life. But at any rate the name 'the British Empire' was accurate.

standstill. When Reed took over IPC, they agreed that they would not sell Butterworths, the legal publishers, to an American firm. No doubt it would turn out, if the question arose, that some other firms are under implicit if not explicit protection from foreign takeovers. But with these few exceptions, takeovers have been permitted and new investments welcomed.

This welcome has derived from the belief that inward investment, particularly American investment, brings to this country new management techniques, new technology, that sometimes it intensifies competition and that frequently it helps exports. Little has been done by governments to supervise or monitor these effects but it does not seem at all unreasonable to believe that they do occur. The UK has a particular reason for not being too fussy about inward investment. The UK is itself a large overseas investor. It does not want to stir up trouble for itself abroad by giving a bad example of rigid control over investment coming into the UK, and although UK companies frequently find conditions imposed upon them by the governments of the countries in which they invest, the UK government has not in general wished to follow suit. It has abstained from action.

If the costs of inward investment are small relative to the benefits, it would certainly be a strong argument for a country investing abroad to the extent the UK does to let sleeping dogs lie. It is questionable, however, whether the costs have been as small as has sometimes been thought. Take first the effect on the competitive situation. There are undoubtedly cases where inward investment has increased or even created competition in the British market. Thus, for example, the American firm Air Products has successfully challenged the monopoly of British Oxygen Company in the supply of oxygen. Yet an effect, and probably an intention, of overseas investment in certain cases is to enable large firms to control the competitive situation in their home market. The American dominance of the European motor car industry obviously has this effect. Exports of cars from Europe to the USA are to a considerable degree under American control. The anxiety of American firms to be able to invest freely in

Japan may be motivated in part by a desire to share in the expansion of the Japanese economy, and even to do good to the Japanese. It may also in certain cases have as an object the degree of control over Japanese competition in the American market that such investments might provide. Indeed to the degree that American production becomes less competitive, the more are American firms likely to seek ways of influencing foreign competition in the US market.

Certainly the United States Congress has had it in mind that the competitive situation in the USA might be affected by the behaviour of American companies investing abroad. American Anti-Trust legislation extends to foreign commerce. It has been provided that the merging of American sub-sidiaries abroad is as subject to that legislation as would be the merging of their parent companies in the USA. The American legislation thus provides protection against a merger of Ford, Vauxhall, and Chrysler-Rootes in the UK. From the point of view of the Americans, this legislation may serve—as far as legislation can—to preserve competition in the USA. US subsidiaries abroad will, if they export to the USA, have to compete with each other just as their American parents have to do. But from the point of view of the UK the American dominance of the motor car industry means that the structure and exports of a major industry are subject to foreign control. American firms may in fact show an excellent export record, but no British government can determine, though it may to some extent be able to influence, policy decisions of American parent companies as to which of their subsidiaries should supply particular markets. It may work out well for Britain. It may be working out so well that it is better to leave things alone. There may in any case be by now little choice in the matter. But there are costs here in the form of dependence and uncertainty which might not have been incurred if all this could have been calculated in advance. Certainly the Japanese have been markedly unwilling to incur these costs.

IBM manufactures components in many countries of Western Europe. In this way the company hopes to show regard for the separate national interests within Europe as well as to achieve an economic scale of production. An IBM computer sold or leased in Europe will therefore contain components of many national origins. It is understood that IBM attempts to ensure that for each country it balances its exports and imports. Is it a satisfactory situation for Britain that in an advanced technology industry such as the computer industry one of the two companies that dominate the UK market should strive only to break even? Of course there are gains to the UK from IBM technology and management skills. The point is that there are also costs.

The competitive situation in the UK can be affected in another way. There can be so many American companies competing within the UK on the basis of American technology and American research and development, that it becomes very difficult indeed to build up a strong UK industry with a sufficient home market as a base either for exports or indeed for adequate research and development. This seems to have happened in some parts of the electronics industry.

In recent years attention has been focused on another aspect of the functioning of multinational companies. There has always been the problem of leads and lags from which a currency in distress was likely to suffer. Multinational companies control considerable funds in different countries. Their inter-company trade in their own products and components means that at any one time there is vast inter-company indebtedness. They could hardly refrain from locating their funds and timing their inter-company payments in a way which took account of the likely future of particular national currencies. The answer of course is to ensure that one's currency is not in distress. But that has its own problems even for the most powerful countries and these problems are made more difficult by the additional uncertainties introduced by these multinational operations. Here therefore is another cost.

Mr L. E. J. Brouwer, then senior Managing Director of Royal Dutch Shell, was quoted in the *Financial Times* on 6 March 1970 as saying: 'The only "power" which our internationalism gives us is the ability to choose where and when we will invest.' One might ask what other power any international company would want! It is frequently suggested that the labour relations in the UK are a deterrent to inward investment. Apparently to qualify for such investment, as well as winning the competitive battle in aids of various kinds such as investment incentives, nations are now also to be judged in a docility contest. But can a government accept that the economic future of its nation shall be determined in this way, because what is clearly implied by the free operations of multinational companies is that once a country begins to have difficulties, for example its rate of economic growth slows, its labour relations begin to deteriorate, important international factors will be operating not as a corrective but as an additional penalty of failure.

These are the costs of multinational operations which have to be set against the benefits. It is certainly easier to leave the matter to chance, to hope that in fact the benefits do exceed the costs, that indeed, as is widely believed in the case of the UK, they exceed the costs by a considerable margin. There is moreover the problem that we have been open to inward investment over a long period and that much of the structure of our trade and industry has been determined by it. There may as a result be little of significance that can be done in established industries which will not, in the short term at least, have much higher costs than benefits. Yet where it is possible for the government to intervene in a way which clearly influences the balance of advantage and disadvantage in our favour it would be surprising if such action were not taken. The least the government should do is to monitor the results of inward investment. The Inland Revenue no doubt ensures that normal profits are made and taxed in the UK. Where a new industry, such as North Sea oil, is being developed, government action again seems appropriate to ensure the maximum UK advantage from the operations within our territory of the multinational oil companies. There have been the few cases already mentioned where conditions have been imposed on foreign takeovers. These conditions have related to such matters as the number of British directors on the board, the confirmation of expansion plans, guarantees regarding employment, policies regarding exports. No systematic procedure was, however, established to review the operation of these conditions. In the Chrysler takeover of Rootes, an arrangement was made for IRC financial participation with the right to nominate one director to the board as long as it held its securities in Rootes. In the granting of licences for the exploration of the UK section of the Continental Shelf, conditions have also been imposed regarding such matters as the rate of exploitation, landing in the UK, incorporation of the applicant in the UK, the applicant's contribution to the UK balance of payments, and participation by the Gas Council and NCB. Some conditions have been varied with each round of licensing but they all have this at least in common, that despite the *laissez-faire* instinct British governments are not prepared to leave to market forces or to chance the rate at which economic advantage accrues to the nation from this raw material. Nations have typically been very nationalistic in their attitude to the exploitation of expendable raw material resources. Norway notably has taken a strongly nationalistic line on the exploitation of Norwegian oil. There have been accusations that the UK on the contrary has been very weak with the multinational oil companies, that there is an insufficient public sector share in the exploitation of North Sea oil, and that British manufacturers have not gained sufficiently, as suppliers of industrial goods, from the discovery of North Sea oil.

Preference for British manufacturers would be difficult to reconcile with the spirit and probably also the words of international agreements outlawing discrimination in trade. Yet Mr Tom Boardman, Minister for Industry, said on 19 September 1972: 'The Government will certainly wish to see that British firms are given the full and fair opportunity to compete for orders, *and we shall take into account the performance of oil companies in this respect in allocating future licences.*'[2] These words are hardly a battle-cry but they do show that, at least to this extent, North Sea oil is regarded as an appropriate case for government intervention to maximise UK advantage by calculated action despite international

2 DTI Press Release—my italics.

agreements. But if this is right in the case of oil, it cannot in principle be wrong to seek to maximise national advantage in other industries in which multinational companies operate. The *laissez-faire* instinct is being found to be as inadequate a guide to relationships with multinational companies as it is in other aspects of industrial policy.

Intermezzo

The dominating concept in Part One of this book has been the concept of political responsibility. Political responsibility has been accepted by governments despite the persevering survival of the *laissez-faire* instinct. Industrial policy is born of political responsibility. But political responsibility does not provide any clear guide to the public interest. In steering industrial policy by the light of the public interest, analysis will be valuable, but judgment will decide.

The lack of easily applied criteria in industrial policy, the uncertainties of what to do for the best—in situations where political realism demands that one attempts to do something good and worthy to benefit society—throw much weight on the problems of achieving clear and unambiguous communications between all of the participants in industrial policy—ministers, civil servants, businessmen, employees and the general public. These characteristics of industrial policy demand an efficient system of management to ensure that good decisions are made, responsibilities are clearly defined, and policies efficiently discharged. Some of the problems in achieving all of these are described in Part Two. Some better solutions than at present we appear to possess are then proposed.

Part Two

THE CONDUCT OF
INDUSTRIAL POLICY

E

Chapter 5

THE PROBLEM OF DIALOGUE

1. *The Communication Problem*

It would seem an unexceptionable proposition that British government exists to promote British interests, and therefore to promote the interests of industry to the extent that they are consistent with the public interest in Britain.

But it was argued in Chapter 2 that the public interest is an elusive concept. One might therefore expect that there would be constant communication between British government and British industry in order to identify the public interest in different situations, and to discuss and agree the best method of promoting it.

Such communications are not without problems. One difficulty is that however much regard a British government—of whatever complexion—may pay to the interests of British industry, those interests may not be found invariably identical with the public interest. There may be problems in each side comprehending what the other is after; and when the Labour Party is in power there are, inevitably, special difficulties in achieving understanding. The communication problem has a number of sources:

(*a*) The need to 'manage' the economy.
(*b*) Confusion as to the location of responsibility.
(*c*) Political attitudes.
(*d*) The tendency of businessmen to express righteous thoughts.
(*e*) The 'General Motors' syndrome.
(*f*) The voluntaristic syndrome.
(*g*) The idea of public ownership.
(*h*) Suspicion of civil service attitudes.

(a) *The need to 'manage' the economy.* It frequently appears to industry—to the nationalised sector as much as to the private sector—that government is itself far from clear what are the objectives its policies are designed to serve and in which it requires the co-operation of industry. When there are rapid swings of policy from one extreme to another, for example from *laissez-faire* to intervention, from the Industry Act 1971 to the Industry Act 1972, one is entitled to assume that the government has little confidence in either policy, that it is acting simply under pressure and is hoping that one or other may in some unexplained way perform some unspecified task for the benefit of us all.

This lack of clarity and infirmity of purpose has affected the nationalised industries as well as the private sector. At first Mr John Davies preached what might be regarded as an ideally simple philosophy for the handling of relationships between government and the nationalised industries. They were to act commercially and the government was to disengage. This policy proved impractical for two reasons. First, it is difficult for a government to disengage from decisions which involve the use of large resources, and of substantial sums of Treasury money, and which clearly have significant economic and social effects. It is more difficult when those decisions are taken by industries which enjoy, as do some of the nationalised industries, a monopoly or near-monopoly position. The government is inevitably concerned to see that national resources as large as those employed by the nationalised industries are invested to the best effect, that undesirable social effects of policy are mitigated, and that they do operate in accordance with some concept of the public interest. These matters cannot just be left to the boards of the nationalised industries, however expert they may be, and however much one might like to disengage.

But there is a second reason that makes a simple, arm's length, relationship impossible to achieve, a reason that goes far wider than the temporary blindness of an incoming government. This is that governments try to 'manage' the economy. In so doing industry obviously has a vital part to play. To obtain the co-operation of the private sector in its management policies, governments have only influence, incentives and, in certain cases, legislation available for use. But governments have a more direct power over the nationalised industries. If the government is interested in securing some form of control over the rate of increase in prices and incomes, it may seek to control the price decisions and wage settlements of the nationalised industries. These industries are continuously told to act commercially. Yet in a wider interest, they may be told at the same time to hold down prices or to confront wage claims. Such actions may lead to reduced production and to financial losses which their own commercial interest might not dictate.

If the nationalised industries are sometimes confused—as indeed they are—as to what it is the government really wants from them, the position of the private sector is not likely to be any better. The very concept of management of the economy suggests a balance of considerations no one of which may be permanently dominant. At one time a government may put its emphasis on economic growth. At another the emphasis may be on the containment of inflation. The type of co-operation the government wants from industry will depend on its view of the balance of considerations at a particular moment. At one time a government may look to industry to increase its investment; at another to restrict the rise of prices even at some cost to profits and to investment. Indeed governments may be seeking from industry action which, however much it may be in conformity with short-term objectives, such as righting a deficit in the balance of payments, may have serious long-term effects on its competitiveness. Government may be encouraging through advisory agencies, research and development contracts, export services and investment incentives, what by its demand management policies, its counter-inflationary policies, or its exchange rate policy, it is at the same time positively discouraging.

Industry wants to have clear objectives, such as expansion and profitability. It wants to be efficient, to be profitable, to increase productivity, to invest more, to sell more abroad and to be successful. In other words it wants to do all those things that ministers, who are perhaps seeking excuses for their own shortcomings in the failures of industry, frequently exhort it to do.

The statesmen of industry may be very happy exchanging wise words with Prime Ministers and Chancellors of the Exchequer at Number 10 Downing Street, on the balance of considerations that from time to time leads government to divert industry from these simple purposes. But the majority of industry does not want to be an instrument of government policy. It wants to be able to do those things which it thinks it knows how to do without being restricted by the varying requirements of government policy. It may be unreasonable of industry to be so simple-minded. But governments will allow optimism to triumph over experience if they think they can ignore the vexation that their changes in direction cause in industry. The problem may be insoluble but it should be recognised. Relations should not be exasperated by preaching on either side that ignores the reality of the problem.

(b) *Confusion on the location of responsibility.* Relations between government and industry were probably never worse than after the devaluation on 18 November 1967. The government thought that the additional competitiveness and profitability of our manufactured products—consequences of devaluation which the CBI seemed unable to understand—should have a rapidly favourable effect on the level both of our imports and our exports. Such a dramatic turnround in our affairs did not occur. There were eighteen months of deep anxiety before the swing into surplus occurred. Industry blamed government for mishandling the nation's economy, government blamed industry for lacking the energy and the productive capacity to exploit the opportunity created by devaluation. Government seemed to think that industry should have put in additional capacity in anticipation of devaluation, while industrialists could be heard asserting acidly that they might have done just that if government had given them two years' notice of its intention.

There were many reasons for the bitterness that existed

between government and industry after devaluation. One important reason was the feeling among some leaders of industry that it might not have happened if the CBI had been taken by government into some sort of 'partnership'. There is in fact no evidence at all to justify any such belief. There had been intensive consultation between government and CBI. On the contrary, the whole incident illustrates the misunderstandings that can arise out of attempts by government, legitimate in themselves, to associate the two sides of industry with it in the running of the country. The responsibility of government is in fact indivisible.

Eleven months before devaluation, Mr John Davies as Director-General of the CBI had said this:

> Here we stand today—or so it seems to me—gazing with some disillusionment at one another: Government perplexed that its benevolent enthusiasm should be so lukewarmly reflected and management vexed to find that all that is expected of it is maximum disclosure but no participation in decision. . . . What it seems to me is needed is the replacement of the concept of consultation—which has become practically and rightly a dirty word—by one of partnership.[1]

Yet there was not one word in Mr Davies' speech which suggested that the CBI, if it were taken into such a partnership in decision-taking by the government, could in any way share responsibility for the consequences of the decisions. Indeed, how could it? How can any voluntary association such as the CBI share responsibility with the government? The CBI may feel that it has responsibilities not just to its members but to the nation. The TUC may feel the same. If either or both of them feel that the policies of government are in the national interest, they may be prepared to co-operate in making them work and so discharge the responsibility that they feel towards the national interest. But if those policies fail it will not be they who are held electorally responsible but the government of the day. Governments must therefore retain the right, having received the maximum possible co-operation

[1] The Inaugural Sir George Earle Memorial Lecture: Industry and Government, 13 December 1966 (IERF)

from outside bodies, to decide on national policy. Certainly they must consult—even if Mr Davies still considers that a dirty word. Certainly it is helpful if the government's decisions are acceptable and governments may sometimes be prepared to make concessions in order to make their decisions acceptable, especially if there will then be wider co-operation in making them work. But it only causes confusion about the respective roles and responsibilities of government and industry if any suggestion is made that there can be anything like equal partnership and responsibility.

This confusion of roles was compounded by a statement made by Mr Heath on 26 September 1972 after discussions at Chequers with the TUC and CBI about the possibility of a voluntary prices and incomes policy. He said this: 'What we have really embarked upon is the management of the economy by three parties, the Government, the CBI and the TUC. Of course, the Government has direct responsibilities but both other parties recognised that they have responsibilities as well.'[2]

There is a sense in which these words are justified. If the CBI co-operates in holding down prices and if, in reciprocity, the TUC co-operates in restraining wage demands, they are both in some sense participating in the management of the economy. Moreover it would be absurd to suggest, as does Mr Enoch Powell, that such co-operation has fascist implications. All governments have consulted and sought to win co-operation. The reason that they now consult so much more outside Parliament is that the centres of power have moved outside Parliament. Governments therefore want to gain the co-operation of these centres of power. But Mr Heath's phraseology does increase the danger of misunderstanding about the respective roles of government and industry. There can be no equal partnership in responsibility and consequently there can be no equal partnership in decision-making.

Resentment in industry at those inevitable decisions of government that are unpopular will be enhanced if the idea

2 *The Times* 27 September 1972

is created that there can be equal partnership. It was a resentment arising out of such a misunderstanding that promoted the extraordinary outburst of Mr John Davies after devaluation, though he had no better record on that question than had the Labour Government.

(c) *Political attitudes*. It would be wrong to imagine that when government talks to industry it is a conversation between institutions. It is in fact a conversation between individuals. Possibilities of misunderstanding and resentment are therefore greater when there is a Labour government. As individuals and as members of the Labour Party, Labour ministers have political presumptions and ideals which are not shared by the great majority of the leaders of industry. However enthusiastic Labour ministers may be at encouraging the development of the private sector, however much they may consult, however slow they may be in extending the public sector, there is a residuum of doubt and distrust in the minds of industrial leaders. As an unknown Junior Minister I was once taken for a civil servant by the host of a lunch party of businessmen and received condolences on having the task of serving Labour ministers. Even where Labour ministers show themselves understanding of the problems of industry there remains the question of taxation of personal income to act as an irritant in these relationships. As individuals industrial leaders objected to the level of taxation. If they were owners they objected to the close company provisions. If they were senior executives in large firms perhaps with little private capital of their own, they objected furiously to the disallowance of interest on bank borrowings. I remember one industrialist, who had been more friendly and co-operative than most, exploding about the effect of that measure on his standard of living. There was not much that a Labour government could do for industry in general or for his company in particular which would compensate him for the personal consequences of that decision.

Conservative ministers who are not anxious to extend the public sector, and who are known now to believe in substantial reductions in personal taxation, are less likely to encounter this particular hazard in their relations with industry. But there is a sense in which all politicians will find themselves suspect. Few politicians are pure pragmatists. Doctrine is always there lurking in the background—if not sticking out like a sore thumb. They may be pushed off doctrine by the weight of evidence or of public pressures. They will repair to their doctrines and always try to defend themselves in these terms, even in the most extreme circumstances. Thus when Rolls Royce was nationalised by a Conservative government, it was claimed by Conservative ministers that the company would be restored to the private sector once it could stand on its own feet. The likelihood of such a restoration may have been small but it had to be called in aid of a policy directly contrary to Conservative presumptions.

In exactly the same way it was found necessary to conciliate backbench Conservative criticism by amending Mr John Davies' original draft of the 1972 Industry Bill—a bill also in many respects contrary to Conservative presumptions—in order to give assurances that in the course of selective assistance to industry, equity holdings would not be acquired too often or held too long.

Politicians need ideology. They cannot just be practical men. They are in politics for wider purposes than sustaining British industry. They are concerned with the nature of society, and with maintaining it, changing it or conserving its essential principles according to some criteria that they have adopted very much as an act of faith. Even when they are dealing with the problems of industry, they cannot free themselves from an ultimate reliance on ideology of some kind, even if it is only a belief in the benefits of competition or that it is legitimate in some cases for governments to act to save jobs threatened by bankruptcies.

Ministers need ideology, preferably one shared with their ministerial colleagues. Ideology and the ideological concurrence of their colleagues and supporters is the ultimate bolster to their confidence and their decision-making power. But they will be a barrier to discussion with practical men of business. Such men may find it strange to encounter in

government an ideological rather than a pragmatic attitude
to the problems of their companies or industries. They
encounter this strangeness in Conservative governments as
well as in Labour. Some shipbuilders in the earlier days of the
Heath government found the *laissez-faire* ideological presumptions of Conservative ministers rather odd. They did not
feel those attitudes had much relationship to the world as
they knew it. They would no doubt have given warm support
to the general idea of disengagement by government from
industry. But, they felt, the shipbuilding industry was an
exception. No doubt the machine tool industry also felt
itself to be an exception. The computer industry and the
electronic industry certainly did. While aerospace might find
other industries odd that did not carefully organise their
public relations in order to pressurise Members of Parliament
into diverting money from the public coffers to the private
pockets of the industry.

(d) *The tendency of businessmen to express righteous thoughts.*
Businessmen also have ideologies. Keynes has often been
quoted on this point. 'The ideas of economists and political
philosophers, both when they are right and when they are
wrong, are more powerful than is commonly understood.
Indeed the world is ruled by little else. Practical men, who
believe themselves to be quite exempt from any intellectual
influences, are usually the slaves of some defunct economist.'[3] Yet the ideology is usually instinctive rather than intellectual. Not all defunct economists are influential, only
those who have articulated continuing instincts. The *laissez-
faire* instinct provides the criteria by which righteousness is
assessed. Thus businessmen are likely to feel that there is
something suspect about public expenditure. They may even
allow that suspicion to damage their own interests. Keynes
is reported to have said of the 1931 Economy Report of the
May Committee (that committee of practical men called
together to recommend what to do to meet the consequences
of the 1931 economic crisis) that it was 'the most foolish

[3] J. M. Keynes *The General Theory of Employment, Interest and Money*
(Macmillan) p. 383

document I have ever had the misfortune to read'.[4] Keynes wrote of the report: 'The Committee shows no evidence of having given a moment's thought to the possible repercussions of their programme either on the volume of employment or on the receipts of taxation.'[5] The report was not merely contrary to the public interest. It was also contrary to the private interests of its authors and their firms. More recently, the attitude of some industrialists to investment grants, when introduced by a Labour government, was conditioned by a comparable instinctive suspicion.

For reasons no doubt deeply entrenched in the nature of our society, certain thoughts are not respectable and are therefore suppressed. It is wrong, for example, to be too acquisitive. For this reason it is difficult for government and industry to discuss honestly the level of personal taxation. It is apparently not respectable even for businessmen to say: 'I want a higher standard of living and therefore a lower level of taxation.' He feels he has to say: 'I need an incentive to work harder.' Working harder is respectable and therefore the alleged method of achieving it, lower taxation on high incomes, takes on a certain respectability. As will be seen later, similar semantic problems confused understanding about the nature of investment incentives. It was no use Labour ministers, who were regarded as particularly guilty, replying that a high level of personal taxation had in fact been extracted by Conservative governments, or that the eruption of argument about incentives was a very modern phenomenon largely no doubt influenced by the discovery how much better people of equivalent status were doing in the USA and even Western Europe. Leave aside the discourtesy of questioning what was being alleged about incentives and the way businessmen would react to them, the discussion was not really about incentives at all. It was about the level of taxation and about standard of living.

Fortunately, perhaps, businessmen are concerned most of the time with the necessarily rather pragmatic occupation of running their companies. In the end, therefore, it is likely

[4] R. F. Harrod *The Life of John Maynard Keynes* p. 438
[5] ibid.

to be the pragmatic interests of their companies that dominate their minds rather than their ideologies, though it may take a struggle to achieve this. Meanwhile confusion may be caused as to what they really mean. Wilkie Collins described a proper attitude for ideological businessmen when he put in the mouth of one character in his novel *The Moonstone* the words: 'Let your faith be as your stockings, and your stockings as your faith. Both ever spotless and both ever ready to put on at a moment's notice.'

(e) *The 'General Motors' syndrome.* Hence we come to the 'General Motors' syndrome, the conviction typified by the claim that the interests of General Motors are identical with those of the United States. Unfortunately such an open and honest expression of view falls only with difficulty from the embarrassed lips of a British businessman. His natural instinct to that effect is inhibited by his *laissez-faire* instinct, which tells him that such a thought is really rather improper. The pressures of international competition are however increasingly overcoming this reticence. The problem then facing government is to persuade beleaguered businessmen that there is in fact still some truth in the propositions about international competition which British industry in its heyday itself so happily preached.

(f) *The voluntaristic syndrome.* Government is not merely concerned with industry as a producer. It is concerned also to persuade or compel industry to pay the social costs of its activities which may not otherwise appear in the profit and loss account. Thus it is concerned with such matters as redundancy, safety, pollution, congestion, with the behaviour of companies as they affect the amenity of society. The question is how far these matters should be left to the voluntary self-discipline of industry and how far they should be the subject of official regulation. This question throws up disagreement between government and industry and, indeed, within industry.

There are those in industry who believe that industry should act as economic man, subject only to such regulations as governments make for the benefit of society as a whole. Everyone in industry would then know where he stands, by what rules of conduct he should live, and the competitive battle would be in no way distorted by the actions of some industrialists to lower standards or by others to raise them.

It is not, however, this simple view that prevails in industry. Industry, like government, has a mixture of motives and profit is only one, and may not in all cases be the most important. Industrialists may seek by what they do to influence the nature of society as well as contribute towards its wealth. Sir Alfred Mond, the first chairman of ICI, was well known for his view that there were in every country a number of people who for one reason or another were incapable of earning their living, and that it was the duty of ICI as a major British company to employ some of them.

Whether it be paternalism, or a mere self-interested desire to preserve their own sort of society, or a search for personal prestige and position, not all industrialists will be motivated simply by the profit and loss account.

There are other industrialists who will condemn such futile, uncapitalist attitudes. They will find in them reason for our economic failures. They confuse the criteria by which industry should act and they thus lower its efficiency. Let Caesar for one moment be diverted by God's law into standards of behaviour more civilised than those of his enemies, and he will start losing his battles. Thus regulation, social, moral, regional, or environmental, must be equally binding on all and in no case self-imposed.

Yet there may be profit in paternalism. That early British socialist, Robert Owen, was a businessman who created at New Lanark an industrial community which provided not just employment but housing, shopping facilities, and other amenities. Robert Owen also made a profit for his share-holders. There is, after all, profit in having a contented workforce and, if training costs are high, there is profit in having a stable workforce. The example of Robert Owen has been followed in many parts of the world, and especially in less developed countries, by perhaps less idealistic capitalists who have seen advantage in providing for their employees from the cradle to the grave, housing, education, medical services, churches and, inevitably, cemeteries.

Without going as far as Robert Owen, companies may decide to seek profit by raising standards. They may find it advantageous, taking account of known public attitudes, to advertise what they do to avoid pollution and to contribute to the quality of the environment. They may then be led in fact to do more than government rules or legislation require.

Reliance on voluntary action has the advantage of leaving people with experience of particular industries free to point the ways in which the standards of industrial behaviour can be raised. There is no reason in principle to reject it in all cases as the appropriate approach. The fact remains that it has failed again and again. Over an increasingly wide field, government and Parliament have had to intervene. Even where government is content to allow regulation still to take the form of voluntary agreement, as for example in the Takeover Code and Panel, there must be a reserve threat, if not yet a reserve power, in government. The threat of government action can be a powerful ally of voluntary agreement.

Thus in this area too there can be misunderstanding and friction. Some will complain that the voluntary approach has not been given sufficient chance. Others will insist that it is the duty of government to establish by regulation the standards to which it expects industry to adhere.

Government has developed by acquiring capacity for intervention in such matters, it meets considerable criticism when urgent requirements for intervention cannot be urgently met due to lack of administrative capacity, and it is therefore well advised to prepare itself to meet emerging public demand. A government prepared for action is a government on the brink of action. The brink is a dangerous place. Action is safer.

(g) *The idea of public ownership.* Public ownership or equity participation as a condition of government assistance has been

a sensitive issue between businessmen and Labour governments, but not only with Labour governments. It threatens
the independence of industry. It is not the only way in which
government aid can threaten that independence, but it is
the most important.

Public ownership has been a far greater issue in this country
than in other Western European countries; there it has been
possible to consider its appropriateness in particular cases
with far less ideological commitment. Sir Richard Clarke,
former Permanent Secretary to the Ministry of Technology,
has written in *New Trends in Government* concerning the
industries nationalised in Britain under conditions of political controversy: 'Many of these industries are nationalised
in other countries but rarely in circumstances of political
controversy . . . without the background of political interest
and controversy, these industries in other countries tend to
be spared the spotlight that is focused on them here.'[6]

Perhaps this will diminish as a matter of political controversy following the nationalisation of Rolls Royce. On
that occasion Enoch Powell said, 'That is an extraordinary
proposition to come from a Conservative government—that
State ownership is the natural instrument, the chosen method,
for restoring unprofitable assets to profitability.'[7] Perhaps
in future it will seem less extraordinary if such a proposition
comes again from a Conservative government and consequently more acceptable if it comes from a Labour government.

For public ownership, though it is part of a socialist
ideology, may also in certain circumstances be the preferred
means of government aid to an industry or company. The
Conservative government's Industry Act 1972 includes
provision for governments to take equity in private companies. The relevance of ownership to industrial management,
which was being denied fifteen years ago, is now once more
emphasised. Twenty years ago Gaitskell was suggesting that
the divorce between ownership and management could have
beneficial effects, for example on the level of investment:

6 Sir Richard Clarke *New Trends in Government* (HMSO) pp. 73-4
7 House of Commons, Official Report, vol. 811 col. 82

'Recent experience suggests on the whole that partly because of the divorce between ownership and control in industry, partly because of fiscal incentives, it may not be so difficult to ensure a continuous readiness to invest by business executives even if the government is pursuing egalitarian policies.'[8] In more recent years, however, there has been much emphasis on the neglected potentiality of ownership to improve industrial performance. There has been pressure, for example, on large shareholders such as insurance companies to act as the banks are reported to act in Germany, to bring pressure on industrial management to achieve better performance. If a remarriage between ownership and management is now considered so desirable, ownership must be one option of government when it sees the need to intervene to assist industry.

But such an attitude, even if practically and not ideologically based, is not acceptable to the ideology of most British businessmen. It is more readily accepted when there is a Conservative government because it is understood that Conservatives have no ideological commitment to extending the public sector. When there is a Labour government, any extension of the public sector, however pragmatic the motivation, is likely to provoke hysteria. In recognition of that attitude, and out of fear that its worth would be impeded if it was believed to be an instrument of 'backdoor' nationalisation, the Labour government made it clear that the Industrial Reorganisation Corporation, though it could hold a company's equity, would not hold it indefinitely. Repudiation of the intention to use the IRC as an instrument of public ownership did not however free it from suspicion. The CBI reacted with high ideological indignation and with even higher indignation to the Labour government's Industrial Expansion Bill. Mr John Davies, as Director General of the CBI, refused even to discuss the Bill with Labour ministers to see if any accommodation of views was possible.

There was, therefore, some irony in the fact that it was Mr John Davies who, as Secretary of State for Trade and

[8] Hugh Gaitskell *Socialism and Nationalisation* (Fabian Tract 300) p. 34

Industry, introduced in 1972 an Industry Act creating powers of selective acquisition of equity going far beyond anything in the Industrial Expansion Act of 1968 and, even after amendment, with substantially less parliamentary control than had been provided in the Industrial Expansion Act. The CBI in 1972 did not break off relations with the government of the day. It allowed itself to be satisfied by some fairly nominal amendments to the original Bill. These increased parliamentary control and introduced some safeguards against too enthusiastic a conversion by the Conservative Government to the merits of equity participation.

The CBI then gave its presidential blessing *urbi et orbe* (to the City of London and to the world). It is not a surprising characteristic of the CBI that whatever difficulties businessmen have in understanding the ideologies of politicians, even Conservative politicians, it does feel more trust in a Conservative government than in a Labour government. But perhaps even the CBI is becoming a little more pragmatic in its attitude to public ownership.

(h) *Suspicion of civil service attitudes.* There is a sense in which the Queen's government is carried on from decade to decade and is unaffected by the political mortality of particular parties and Prime Ministers. The Queen's government is carried on and the Civil Service is permanent.

When businessmen speak to government they normally speak not to ministers but to civil servants. Some businessmen claim to detect in government at the official level an impartiality between British and foreign interests which is difficult to stomach. The Civil Service is believed to constitute a brotherhood so far above the anxieties of ordinary life that it cannot be relied on either for urgency or for commitment to British interests.

If, for example, one believes one's foreign competitors guilty of dumping in one's home market, one will find the Department of Trade and Industry acting with a judicial impartiality, carefully examining the evidence, carefully assessing the damage actually done. In the end they will probably turn one's case down either because they cannot prove something that to you is obvious or because they have decided that in the overall national interest it would be better not to impose anti-dumping duties. After all if this country acts unreasonably against dumping there may be retaliation which may be more costly than the benefits of anti-dumping action; and in any case we are bound by international agreement to proceed on dumping on the basis of a careful review of the evidence, not on the basis of protective nationalism. But none of this is much consolation if you suspect your competitors of selling to your customers at prices below your raw material costs.

The picture many businessmen have of civil servants as above the battle is a caricature. It is nevertheless influential and it creates resentment. This resentment is sometimes given an outlet by means of an appeal to a minister against his own civil servants. Ministers are then found normally to be reluctant to overrule their civil servants. Indeed there may be worse to follow than the mere failure of an appeal to the minister which was not really expected to succeed anyhow, for do not all ministers end up as prisoners of their civil servants? The worse that may be to come is a polite exhortation that will help the petitioners on their way as they leave the ministerial office. Ministers may be undermining one's home market by allowing dumped imports, or by deflationary measures that cut sales of durable goods. They may thus be making everything more difficult—investment because it is more risky, and productivity because, in the absence of a reliably expanding market, it is likely to cause redundancy which the trade unions will understandably oppose. But one should not expect to be able to depart from the minister's august presence without hearing from him something of the advantages of greater efficiency, more investment and higher exports. There are civil servants who are particularly adept at drafting little homilies of this kind. And there are ministers who, even in the most unsuitable circumstances, show themselves quite unable to resist any temptation to teach grandmother to suck eggs.

It is fair to say that, particularly no doubt when there is a Labour government, industrialists miss few opportunities of educating ministers in such matters as the key role of profit in a capitalist economy. These helpful exchanges of useful information on the sucking of eggs can shorten tempers.

2. *Investment Incentives*

The Bolton Committee on Small Firms said: 'there appears to be a tendency to mistrust initiatives of Labour governments on principle and irrespective of their merits'.[9] This is as true of large firms as of small firms. Investment grants were introduced by a Labour government. They were therefore greeted with instant opposition, irrespective of merit, just as was the Regional Employment Premium.

Previously investment incentives had been in the form of allowances against tax. The Labour government introduced investment grants in 1966 because it was thought that grants would be a more effective form of investment incentive than allowances had been. The argument was pragmatic, not ideological. It was an unlikely ideological cause for a Labour government to pay cash grants to private industry. This story illustrates admirably the problems of achieving understanding between a Labour government and industry.

Investment allowances bring benefit only after a profit has been made on the actual cost of the capital investment. Investment grants act directly to reduce the cost of capital investment. They thus make investment cheaper and profit easier to make. Despite these attractions, and pressure from industry for effective investment incentives, much of industry and particularly the CBI disliked investment grants. One objection was that they were in fact operated in a selective manner to assist manufacturing industry but not services or distribution. This characteristic of the grants system was not inherent in it, and there was no reason in principle why grants should not have been used to assist investment in services and distribution. But it was thought better to concentrate assistance on that part of the economy which was lagging most and which found itself in keenest competition, at home and abroad, with foreign competitors. This reasoning was not

[9] Report of the Committee of Inquiry on Small Firms (HMSO) p. 93 para 9.3

accepted, particularly by those in industry who lost by it, and it served to damn the grant system with the opprobrium of 'selectivity' which, for other reasons, was then regarded as a particular hallmark of a Labour government's 'socialistic' policies. Since then, selectivity has become a hallmark of a Conservative government's policies too, including discrimination against services and distribution. Mr John Davies' justification of that discrimination during debates on the Industry Act 1972 could have been argued by any Labour minister between 1966 and 1970.

A second objection was that grants could be obtained for the benefit of projects that might never make a profit. The fact that even at the highest (development area) rate of grant, the majority of the money would still have to come from private interests which would demand a return on their investment, was not accepted as an answer to this criticism. The Labour government was thought to be suspicious of profit-making and the profit motive, and was suspected of having introduced grants because they were an incentive not dependent on profitability for their effect.

The grant system was also criticised on the grounds that it gave its principal aid to capital intensive investment and that the development area differential was paid without any regard to new employment actually created. This of course was true, but it was also true of an investment allowance system. Indeed one argument produced by the CBI in favour of having investment incentives at all rather than a straight reduction in company taxation, was precisely to give special assistance to capital intensive investment. This particular argument was not one against the grant system alone but against any system in which the incentive was directly related to the size of the capital expenditure and which took no account of employment actually created or maintained. At least the Labour government introduced in the development areas a regional employment premium which was related to the actual number of people employed. In the Industry Act 1972 the Conservative Government abolished all statutory linkages between development area assistance and the direct creation of new employment. No objection was heard from industry.

One of the grant system's great merits in the view of the government was its 'transparency', the fact that it was clear to everyone including a works manager how it worked, whereas a tax allowance system was comprehensible to accountants and few others. Even this was denied to it on the grounds that whatever the intention, its selectivity made it difficult to understand. In one sense it was held to be too transparent. The government and the public are very much more aware of public expenditure than of rebates against taxation. Public expenditure on grants was high and not easily forecastable. The CBI in particular feared that as government and public became aware of this growing expenditure competing with other forms of public expenditure of high priority, investment incentives for industry would be sacrificed to increased social expenditure.

Undoubtedly in the investment grant system as it was introduced, there were serious administrative disadvantages. Even the government would not have denied that administratively it was more burdensome than tax allowances. But many firms with investment projects which were large in relation to their current size or their current profits found the system advantageous. It was precisely firms willing to undertake such rapid expansion that a system of incentives should be designed to encourage.

There was as a matter of fact one rather striking piece of evidence as to the advantages of the investment grant system, the hostility of our foreign competitors. Their objections derived not from any idea that grants were ineffective but from the fear that they were too effective for the comfort of Britain's competitors. It is not often that British businessmen rush so enthusiastically to the support of their foreign rivals. It was in large part the hostility of British businessmen that led to the abolition of the grant system in October 1970 by the new Conservative government.

In due course the Conservative government itself reintroduced investment grants in development areas under another name. Presumably this was done because that government had decided that grants were an effective method of encouraging industrial expansion in development areas.

But the effectiveness of grants as a system of investment incentive did not protect them against the hostility of much of industry and of the official spokesmen of industry when a Labour government introduced them.

The instinctive wisdom of businessmen told them that investment grants were bad in principle, despite the fact that they were often seen to be beneficial in practice. Reports such as the Rochdale Committee Report on shipping and the Way Committee Report on machine tools argued for the replacement of investment grants, because whatever their effect in practice they were bad in principle.[10] The reports emphasised the need for government to seek to obtain the same effect by other, presumably more respectable, means! But there was no other way of obtaining the same effect.

Businessmen fell into a kind of schizophrenia as they balanced the benefits of grants against the philosophical abhorrence in which the received wisdom dictated they should be held. This melancholy condition was illustrated by one spokesman of the Chamber of Shipping after investment grants had been abolished. This spokesman had delivered a strong speech attacking the government's decision. It had greatly weakened the shipping industry and its international competitiveness. He subsequently told me in private that the government was of course quite right in what it had done because investment grants, whatever their beneficial effect, were objectionable in principle!

There is a tail-piece to this story of instant opposition. Precisely because there were certain companies which benefited greatly from the grant system, the CBI, which had opposed the grant system throughout, was placed in some difficulty when the new Conservative government decided to abolish it. The difficulties of the CBI were no doubt a great deal less than they deserved to be, because of the philosophic prejudice against grants even of businessmen who had gained from them. Yet some companies were going to lose and the CBI had to find some way of speaking for all its members. A

[10] Rochdale was influenced by the abuse of investment grants by foreign-owned, British-registered, shipping companies. There were other ways of handling these abuses than by abolishing the grant system.

remarkable compromise was worked out as the basis of the CIB's submission to government. Grants should be abolished except for companies who were going to lose. For those companies grants should be retained!

The CBI failed to argue the case that eventually in 1972 did become persuasive with government, that there should be grants in development areas as a supplement to tax allowances in the country generally. Nevertheless, the CBI had at length discovered some companies for whom cash was more important than principle and at the eleventh hour had become ready to associate itself with such a view. Thus the CBI solved its political problem probably at some expense to its credibility with a new government filled with ideological fervour against investment grants.

It is an unexpected and even disappointing characteristic of government–industry relations that the politicians on the industry side may be even more elusive than the politicians in government, and that by the time the decisions of principle come to be made, the politicians of industry are found to be hedging their bets.

3. *Textile Tariffs*
Even where there is unanimity between government and industry as to what should be done, and even when the most elaborate consultations are held, the outcome can cause disappointment and frustration, and can reveal misunderstandings that subsequently sour relations. The textile tariff decision of the summer of 1969 is a good example (about which Arthur Knight has written extensively in his companion volume).

In the summer of 1969, Anthony Crosland, President of the Board of Trade, decided to impose a tariff in place of quotas on imports of cotton textiles from the Commonwealth. The tariff was to operate as from 1 January 1972.

Tariffs and quotas are each of them methods of protecting domestic industry. A quota places an absolute limit on imports. The effectiveness of a tariff depends on its level and on the relative competitiveness of domestic and foreign products. Thus a tariff can be more or less protective than a quota, depending on the relative efficiency of the domestic industry.

Crosland's decision was taken on the advice of the Textile Council. That advice implied a belief that the Lancashire textile industry could achieve, by the date on which the quota was to be abolished and the tariff introduced, a level of efficiency sufficient to flourish behind the new form of protection. The Textile Council had been asked three years before by the Board of Trade to prepare a report on the productivity and efficiency of the Lancashire textile industry. The report was prepared by the Textile Council in consultation with Board of Trade officials, and it was a document for which the Textile Council took full responsibility.

The report accepted that there would be a severe run-down in employment in the industry over the following years as an inevitable result of closures, higher productivity, and capital intensive investment.

There were recommendations, based on most careful study, as to how to achieve rationalisation and higher efficiency in the industry. 'We believe labour productivity in the industry can and must be doubled by 1975', said Section IV of the Report dealing with labour.

The Report was not quite unanimous. Mr Edmund Gartside dissented from the recommendation that from 1 January 1973 control of cotton textile imports from Commonwealth countries should be by tariff at the Commonwealth preferential rate rather than, as previously, by quota. Mr Gartside apart, not merely the management of the industry but the trade unions went along with the idea that much higher efficiency was obtainable and that a tariff from 1 January 1973 at the level proposed would be adequate protection against cheap imports.

Lord Kearton, Chairman of Courtaulds, wrote in a confident article in *The Times* (1 April 1969): 'Courtaulds and other progressive firms are prepared to have their efficiency judged by international standards, subject to normal duties only, and without the present pattern of United Kingdom quotas.'

It was of course recommended by the Textile Council that

the government should take action to prevent a disruptive rise in imports while the industry was adjusting itself to reliance on tariff protection alone. But it was perfectly well understood in 1969 that the government, while it might agree to replace the quota by a tariff, would not be prepared, in view of its obligations to the Commonwealth, simply to add a tariff to the quota. The government feared that if there were protection by both tariff and quota, it would be very difficult at the end of the transitional period to get rid of the quotas. The leaders of the Textile Council accepted that if there could not be even temporarily both tariff and quota, there should be a tariff instead of the quota. The government indicated that if there was to be a tariff, it would be more convenient if it could be introduced on 1 January 1972 rather than 1 January 1973, as the existing quotas would expire on 31 December 1971. This would reduce the time available to achieve the necessary productivity increases. But the leaders of the Textile Council agreed to that too.

It is no secret that Board of Trade ministers were surprised at the recommendation of a tariff instead of a quota. Experience has shown that it takes a very long time to raise the productivity and efficiency of an industry by the amount calculated in the report as necessary if the textile industry was to compete behind tariff protection alone. It seemed very doubtful whether the textile industry could do so much in so short a time. At a meeting in Manchester with leading figures in the Textile Council such scepticism was met by the firmest and most confident assurances, Edmund Gartside alone dissenting.

The main criticism being made at the time, particularly by those concerned with the problems of less developed countries, was not that the proposal would encourage imports but that it was too highly protectionist. It would damage the export prospects of less developed Commonwealth countries. Particular anxiety was expressed by development experts regarding the problem of India's textile exports to the United Kingdom if it were deprived of its country quota. So when Crosland made his announcement about the introduction of a tariff, he coupled it with an offer to India of additional aid in an attempt to compensate for any loss of trade. Nevertheless Crosland's announcement was assailed as harmful to the interests of the developing world.

Never has any decision in the field of industrial policy been taken in closer concert with industry than was Crosland's decision to substitute a tariff from 1 January 1972. It would have outraged the Lancashire textile industry if any other decision had been taken. But at the beginning of December 1971 the decision was reversed under pressure from the textile industry and it was announced that from 1 January 1972 there would in fact be quotas as well as a tariff. A combination of protective devices which had seemed inconceivable in the summer of 1969 had become actual government policy by the end of 1971. The development experts had been right in their fears as to British intentions, though wrong in their criticism of the tariff proposal. It was not that the tariff was too high but that the protection provided by it was too low. Those were right who argued in the Board of Trade in 1969 that if the government did introduce a tariff, it would not be long before there was both tariff and quota. Crosland himself in his announcement had referred to the possibility of emergency recourse to the GATT long-term agreement, and hence to the use of quotas, if following the introduction of the tariff there was disruption in the industry arising from imports. But that was an ultimate safeguard. The acceptance of the tariff had been on the basis that a tariff would be sufficient.

By the autumn of 1971 many of those gentlemen who in 1969 were prepared to recommend a tariff had disappeared from view. Great firms whose representatives on the Textile Council had in 1969 gone along with the tariff proposal were by 1971 lobbying Members of Parliament for the continuation of the quota. The industry was rallying to the side of Edmund Gartside's Textile Industry Support Council. Gartside himself was the hero of textile Lancashire. The Lancashire textile industry feared it had come nowhere near achieving the increases in productivity and efficiency that would be required to survive behind tariff protection alone. Actual closures and redundancies proved, when they appeared on schedule, more terrifying than forecast closures and redundancies. Trade union leaders who had been prepared to contemplate theoretical redundancies when they only figured in a report, could not but show alarm at actual redundancies when they occurred among their own members.

There were, of course, changes in the world situation since the summer of 1969. Japan had agreed to restrict its textile exports to the United States. This agreement could divert Japanese exports to the United Kingdom. There was very high unemployment in Britain. Our application to join the EEC had succeeded and therefore in any case we were likely in the course of harmonisation to revert to quotas rather than a tariff alone, as our form of textile protection. But whatever influence those arguments had on the sudden change in policy, it was quite clear that the pressure from the industry for that change derived from the textile industry's awakening to the fact that the Textile Council's recommendations had been completely unrealistic. What could one expect, the industry was asking in the autumn of 1971, from a government-nominated body like the Textile Council? What could one expect from all those *laissez-faire*-minded officials in the Board of Trade, than the imposition of an inadequate tariff? If only ministers listened to the industry rather than to their own officials, they would learn sense.

But ministers had listened to the industry. The Textile Council had spoken for the industry. The proposals for change did have the support of the industry, in 1969 if not in 1971. If the government in 1969 had refused to adopt the Textile Council's recommendations, unfavourable reference would have been made to all those *laissez-faire* officials at the Board of Trade who persuaded out-of-touch ministers to reject the representations of the textile industry instead of listening to the industry and introducing a tariff.

There might be some comfort in a situation such as this if one could believe that the leaders of the industry were really rather cleverer than ministers and pushed the tariff idea with a view to ending up with protection by both quota and tariff. There is no evidence of such subtlety. The industry made a mistake and competition forced it into a change of view.

Industry, understandably, wants government to follow the varying path of its fortunes with unfailing care and consolation. If industry makes a mistake and as a result its views change, then government must change. If there are difficulties in this because meanwhile the government has entered into international agreements in implementation of the earlier policy, then someone is to blame, and it is usually officials at the Board with day-to-day contact who take the punishment.

Governments have to live with the consequences of their decisions until the electorate enables them to take refuge in the mingled joy and misery of defeat. Advisers can change their advice with all the rectitude that arises from the wisdom of hindsight, and they stay around longer. If a minister survives long enough to enjoy the privilege of receiving from the same adviser advice directly contrary to that which he was given last time, he may reflect that it is hardly worth drawing attention to so curious a fact. After all, it is his own fault if he took the advice last time. The different advice now being given may prove to be correct. It is his responsibility anyway. There is little point in shooting advisers to encourage the others.

Chapter 6

INTERVENTION AT ARM'S LENGTH

1. *The Civil Service at Arm's Length*

The picture drawn in the previous chapter of misunderstanding and suspicion between business and government is no doubt only part of the truth, but it is an important part. Another important part is the way in which the reluctant attitude of the Civil Service to government intervention in industry has conditioned the form of that intervention when it has occurred.

The Civil Service is a professional career service. It consists of people of high calibre, very few of whom however have any substantial personal experience of industry. In dealing with industry, therefore, they are dealing with activities which they do not fully understand. They are aware how far the successful running of the machinery of government in this country depends on their skill, how important it is that the reputation of the government machine should not be unnecessarily imperilled, and yet how great are the dangers of error if the Civil Service moves beyond its immediate experience. All this adds up to a preference for abstention from intervention. Even regulatory functions, such as those under the Companies and Insurance Companies Acts and the Monopolies and Mergers Acts, are carried out with a reluctance and a lack of conviction attributable to a fear of the consequences of action, including the political consequences. To confirm them in this attitude of abstention is the spectacle of corruption in some countries in which relations between government and industry are known to be closer, and where there is frequent suspicion that contact with government can bring discrimination in one's favour at a price.

Discrimination in favour of particular firms causes a special anxiety. Such discrimination will normally be based on judgment rather than hard evidence; and it may turn out badly and be difficult to justify either contemporaneously or retrospectively. The Civil Service is therefore likely to be particularly reticent in advising ministers to engage in selective intervention unless there can be demonstrated a very clear and virtually unquestioned national interest.

Rightly or wrongly, aerospace has for many years qualified as such a national interest. The computer industry achieved this status about 1965. Regional policy is a third well-established justification for selective intervention. When there exist such virtually unquestioned national interests, the situation changes. There will be within departments, groups of civil servants specially charged with pursuing these interests. Yet even in these cases, as will be seen later, there will be some reluctance to involve government too deeply in the management of industrial activities. Outside such well-established areas of permissible intervention reticence will predominate.

Civil servants will know from bitter experience that politically intervention is more likely to be an embarrassment than a triumph. Therefore their protective attitude to ministers as well as to the government service will recommend caution. There is a long list of catastrophes since the war to prove how government intervention can be both costly and disastrous. Most people's list will start with the groundnuts scheme, continue through the large number of cancelled aerospace projects, will include doubts about the economics of the nuclear programme, and will perhaps end with the evident failure of government to achieve very much through their interventions in the shipbuilding, textile or machine tool industries. Where the political risks are so grave and the possibilities of national advantage so questionable, why get involved? If one has to get involved, why get involved too deeply? Why take management responsibility that can reasonably be left to others? If there is a major collapse threatening large-scale unemployment, and perhaps national prestige or reputation, then at least there is a motive for action. A rescue operation by the government may bring in a political dividend. But why get involved voluntarily? Why convert what sometimes may be a reluctant necessity into a positive policy of intervention, when the dangers are so great and prospective gains so doubtful?

Yet the Civil Service now knows perfectly well that however great its doubts, it will be repeatedly forced to intervene in what it would have wished to be industrial rather than governmental decisions. Any hopes it may have permitted itself to entertain arising out of the initial disengagement policies of the Heath government, must have long since been abandoned. In the past it has demonstrated that, despite Fulton, it has the capacity to adapt itself to new requirements specifically defined. In the Export Credit Guarantee Department, the Civil Service has built up a facility of first-class importance to industry. It has responded very positively to criticism by repeated improvements in the service provided. In the aluminium smelter project the Civil Service showed itself competent to negotiate successfully loan contracts of great complexity. Now that intervention is becoming a bi-partisan way of government in this country, the Civil Service as is its custom will have to set itself to learn from its experience, to acquire the necessary skills or establish the necessary para-governmental agencies, and to advise ministers on how best to handle these undesired but inevitable new tasks. There is some danger, a danger against which the government machine must permanently guard, that when action reluctantly undertaken assumes the character of a routine, much of the care bred of scepticism may disappear. Vested interests will be created within departments and the government machine may not be sufficiently self-critical to exercise the necessary surveillance over the administration of policy.

Thus in a situation where intervention is on the increase, mere reluctance is no protection against misjudgment. Indeed reluctance itself leads to mishandling and misjudgment. It has been responsible for the failure in the past to build up an adequate machinery of surveillance where public money is invested in industry, or at least to consider adequately the implications of the fact that in certain cases, notably in the advanced technology industries, adequate surveillance cannot in the nature of the case be exercised by administrative means. It has led to over-reliance on reports prepared by wise men which have become formalised obstacles to learning, because there has been a lack of confidence in the ability of the Civil Service either to conduct a continuing review of policy or indeed to benefit from the educative processes of actual administration. No consistent line has been drawn between those cases in which the government clearly must act directly and equip itself to do so, and those cases which more appropriately should be handled by some permanent para-governmental agency.

Two illustrations now follow of intervention at arm's length: the RB211 experience and the Geddes Report on Shipbuilding.

2. *The RB211 Experience*

Clear allocation of responsibility is at least as essential when government finance is involved as when a company derives its finance from traditional sources. This is by definition an area of high risk, because otherwise the money would be available from private sources. As it is an area of high risk the quality of management is particularly important. If responsibility is not clearly allocated, assisted firms may be led to surrender into the hands of government responsibilities that their own managements should discharge and which government is not equipped to discharge. Governments have therefore been reluctant to undermine in any way the responsibilities of managers, to confuse responsibility, or to share responsibilities which are not properly theirs to share. They have thought it desirable to limit their financial commitment, because otherwise a firm once it has acquired a place at the public trough may continually come back for more public money with which to pay for its mistakes (for an official statement of this view see Appendix).

In pursuance of this policy, therefore, government has attempted to lay down a line of demarcation between its responsibilities and those of the firm it is helping, and then

F

to hold that line. Thus it has negotiated the aid that seemed necessary at the time, and has then in effect told the assisted firm to get on with it. It has assumed that the firm wishes to succeed or survive, that it has, or has been given, the resources to see the programme through to success, and that therefore all subsequent decisions can be left to its commercial and technical acumen. The most that will be done is to monitor progress through technical or commercial reports, but this is with a view to keeping a check, sometimes giving a second opinion, but not for the purposes of exercising control. The position of the government is frequently little different from that of a shareholder who invests with limited liability on the basis of some sort of prospectus, and then hopes for the best.

The success of such an approach depends on whether, in the last resort, the government can in practice limit its commitment and wash its hands of failure. If it cannot, and if in addition the potential commitment is very large, it will be well advised to face the reality of the situation, accept the fact of unlimited commitment, and draw the appropriate conclusions for the exercise of responsibility.

In 1968 the government decided to give launching aid to the RB211 aero-engine up to 70 per cent of an agreed limit of £65·5 million, leaving 30 per cent and any overruns to Rolls Royce. It did so because it was persuaded that the RB211 was essential to the future of Rolls Royce and that an aero-engine industry was a vital national interest of this country. As Rolls Royce is the national aero-engine industry, the future of Rolls Royce is the future of the industry. This launching aid agreement was the largest ever negotiated by a British government by a very considerable margin. There had been previous launching aid agreement on a fifty-fifty basis. But Rolls Royce's merchant bankers had said that 50 per cent of the estimated development cost was too great a risk for Rolls Royce to accept. Thus there was no doubt that there was considerable risk or that the cost of this development might, even with launching aid, come near the limit of Rolls Royce's own resources. Despite the exceptional size of the launching aid, the government had not even seen the Rolls Royce contract with Lockheed until several months after it was signed, although certain of the key clauses in it were revealed to the government by Rolls Royce as they were negotiated. This was a contract which would, in unfavourable circumstances, be very expensive to Rolls Royce. Yet the government professes to have believed that its own potential liability was limited by the terms of the launching aid agreement.

Sir Robert Marshall, a Permanent Secretary at the Department of Trade and Industry, told the Public Accounts Committee:

It was a very important part of the regime and the relationship between Rolls Royce and the Department that the Company had to bear the risk. The launching aid regime placed the risk of escalation of costs on the Company . . . so that one had that extra measure of reason to suppose that the Company would be most cautious and careful in its estimates of its own costs and its estimates of its own future business.[1]

He repeated later on, 'The Government's decision at that time was that the launching aid arrangements should be taken, and the judgment and the risk should be placed on the contractor. That has not worked out in this particular case.'[2]

The government was taking—and knew it was taking—a risk that it would lose its launching aid. In fact the risk taken by the government was much greater than that. It may not have been foreseen that the contract with Lockheed could bring a firm like Rolls Royce to disaster, but the actual risk taken by the government was that it would have to rescue both Rolls Royce and the contract with Lockheed. Yet because the company, under the terms of the launching aid agreement, took the risk of escalation and because the apparent risk taken by the government was limited, the firm was left to make its own commercial judgments.

[1] Third Report of the Committee of Public Accounts 1971-2 p. 184 Q. 1408
[2] ibid. p. 222 Q. 1702

The problems faced by governments in making this type of arrangement are not easy. It would be absurd if a government, in order to exercise greater control, had to build up a technical and commercial staff as large as the one on which it was checking.

Yet it is also absurd if a government enters into an agreement in the belief that the form of the agreement limits its liability when in fact it does nothing of the sort. If in a particular technological adventure the government risk is small, or at least is limited to the value of the launching aid, a minimal degree of oversight during the implementation of the agreement may be appropriate. If the government's liability is unlimited or very much larger than the figure in the agreement, a very much keener oversight becomes an appropriate option. If a government has decided, or might be expected to decide, that the survival of a particular company is a matter of vital national interest, that in itself implies a great deal for the extent of its commitment, especially if it encourages costly new developments at the frontiers of knowledge.

One can imagine circumstances in which a government might decide, because for example of its confidence in the management of a particular company or because it had no choice, not to exercise detailed oversight even when there was in fact, if not in form, unlimited liability. But at any rate the government should know what it is doing, that its commitment is unlimited, and that the fact that it has decided not to exercise detailed oversight in no way reduces its responsibility should things go wrong.

One hesitates to believe that in the RB211 launching aid agreement, the government could really have imagined that its liability was limited by the form of the agreement. It might imagine that its liability was limited by the technical, managerial and financial resources of Rolls Royce to see the thing through, but surely not by the words of an agreement.

The government machine was in fact unprepared to manage the RB211 commitment. Its lack of preparation was due partly to the fact that the cost of aero-engine development and the technical risks had escalated far beyond previous experience. But to some extent the lack of preparation was the result of deliberate past policy. The government machine has always wished to limit its participation and to demarcate exactly the extent of its responsibility. It has been not unreasonably sceptical of its ability to exercise surveillance beyond the point of demarcation and has believed that it should not be required to do so.

The attitudes which lead the government machine to try where it can to limit its commitment are in themselves entirely reasonable. The dilemma arises where the government of the day decides to enter into commitments which cannot be limited, where responsibility cannot in practice be divided and where the government machine has not, as a matter of fact, the capacity to exercise the necessary surveillance. Governments may nevertheless decide to go ahead. They may decide that the national interest dictates their accepting these higher risks. It seems less likely that ever again will such risks be accepted simply on the basis of one firm's past reputation for the successful management of great projects. But it should not be imagined that lessons learned from the RB211 affair are complete protection against repetition of this type of risk. If the government is to continue financing major technological developments at the frontiers of knowledge, it will do so knowing that it can control the expense only by cancellation and that if cancellation is not possible it cannot control the expense. No doubt minor but useful improvements will be introduced in control systems. But these will not avoid the government becoming the milch cow of advanced technology, as in the case of Concorde. With the RB211 the government's liability appeared to be limited because Rolls Royce nominally shouldered the responsibility for any escalation in development costs. With Concorde no firm would even pretend to share the liability, and there has never been any doubt that the choice facing the government was escalation or cancellation.

The national interest in technological leadership is a great destroyer of commercial disciplines and of attempts by government to limit its responsibility by acting at arm's length. Nor is there really any answer, whatever the pretence of control. It is in fact rather like fighting a war. The cost of fighting a war is large, cannot be forecast and is charged to the government.

There was a time under the first Queen Elizabeth, when the cost of ammunition was debited against the pay of the soldier who fired it. Perhaps it was thought that this would be an incentive for the soldier to shoot with greater accuracy. It was eventually realised that this was not a workable way of winning wars. The cost of wars cannot be controlled by means of financial inducements to one's own side. So it is proving to be in the construction of aircraft.

3. *The Geddes Report on Shipbuilding*

In many ways the problem of managing the government's relations with the shipbuilding industry are parallel to those with Rolls Royce. Similar dilemmas have arisen, and a similar inability to find an answer. But, unlike the Rolls Royce affair, the government's recent involvement with shipbuilding started with a major study of the industry by an independent committee appointed by government.

No doubt under any system of government it is occasionally useful to get a committee of experienced outsiders to take a look at an outstanding problem and report upon it. But under our system of government such reports proliferate. The reports are not asked for as quick checks on continuing policies but as fundamental reviews, often taking a great deal of time, and intended to provide new answers. They are presumably asked for either because the Civil Service has no time to make such reviews or because there exists some doubt as to the capacity of the Civil Service to provide new answers, or because it is believed that the Civil Service is too committed to a particular view to provide new answers. In these reports there are attempts to establish criteria by which policy can be operated for a considerable period ahead. But inevitably they are greatly influenced by current climates of opinion on the handling of industrial problems, as well as by current trends in business. They can only too easily become outdated without anyone noticing because it would require a new report to establish the fact that the emperor no longer had any clothes. This is not a service the Committee can perform because it is disbanded on delivering its report and has no responsibility for implementing any recommendations the government may accept.

Those appointed to prepare such reports labour from the start under the difficulty that they are working in a political ambience without having the experience—or perhaps the wish—to take account of important political considerations which will influence the government's eventual action. They may well feel that they can separate the political factors from the other factors, and that they should propound the best solution ignoring the political factors. But if they do this, their labours are only too likely to be lost. On the other hand, if they try to think themselves into the political aspects of the problem which after all are part—and may be an important part—of the problem, they can easily get it wrong through lack of experience. The Civil Service do have the advantage of spending their lives in a political environment. They can always discuss problems with the minister. They therefore have a chance of recommending the best solution given his political presumptions. A group of outsiders is unlikely to have this assistance even if it wants it. Terms of reference can be drafted to help with this dilemma, except that ministers may not wish to write an insufficiently considered political judgment into the terms of reference. They may in fact require the report to help them make up their minds on the politics. So really this dilemma is inescapable.

The report of the Shipbuilding Inquiry Committee 1965-66 (the Geddes Report) was not one of the worst of such reports. On the contrary it was one of the best, and in many respects it was a pathfinding report. There had been a continuing crisis in shipbuilding, and the Geddes Committee was set up in 1965 to report and make recommendations. It did so in the commendable time for such reports of one year. Nevertheless it illustrates the difficulties with this type of static appraisal of industrial problems.

The report justified government aid to the shipbuilding industry by the prospect of its achieving competitiveness. 'It is this prospect of British shipbuilding being competitive which, in our view, constitutes the case for government action to assist it.'[3]

It rejected any suggestions that the UK must have a merchant shipbuilding industry as a support for our merchant fleet, or to avoid the danger of a Japanese monopoly in shipbuilding, or for defence or balance of payments reasons. The Committee noted that the biggest shipbuilding concerns were concentrated in the regions with above average unemployment. But it concluded that 'In the long run these regions need competitive industries . . . we would not therefore think it right or consistent with general government policy to prop up an industry which is not competitive.'[4]

The system proposed to improve the competitiveness of the industry was 'grouping', that is mergers, the current nostrum for all industrial problems. The recommendation was by no means irrelevant to the problems of the industry. But in fact policy succumbed to the temptation of making grouping an end in itself. Firms outside groups could gain only very limited assistance whatever qualities or prospects they might have. A nostrum 'grouping' was thus elevated to be a condition of aid more important than the fact that some ungrouped yards might have very good prospects of being competitive within their own range of production. The time permitted subsequent to grouping to achieve competitiveness was totally unrealistic. All assistance was to be provided at latest by the end of 1971 and preferably by the end of 1970. The Committee's motive in proposing such a timetable was to bring the necessary pressure on the industry to act. The motive was, perhaps, commendable. But not all problems had been resolved by the end of 1971, nor was it ever likely they could be. The Committee's industrial experience might have warned it that realising productivity and efficiency gains from grouping is not simple and takes time.

The Committee suggested that in order to assist competitiveness, shipbuilding should have a concessionary price for steel. Indeed they came near suggesting that if that was not done, little else would be of value. They had no evidence that

3 Shipbuilding Inquiry Committee 1965-66 Report (HMSO) para. 499
4 ibid. para. 497

this recommendation would be acceptable to the government or to the steel industry, and they did not consider the implications of the non-implementation of the recommendation. Did they really mean that if the government and the steel industry decided against a concessionary price for steel, the government should abandon the shipbuilding industry?

The Report thus doffed its cap in the direction of an acceptable criterion for government aid—competitiveness. It allowed itself to be dominated by a fashionable theory, grouping, in laying down conditions for aid. It proposed a totally unrealistic timetable. It ignored the consequences of any failure, even as Mr John Davies might now call it, non-culpable failure, to achieve competitiveness within the time-scale it had laid down. In addition it assumed that any rundown in employment in the shipbuilding industry would be gradual rather than catastrophic. This led on to the questionable assumption that governments could ignore or cope with any likely redundancies.

The instrument of change in the industry was to be a Shipbuilding Industry Board. The Board was to be in charge of the aid programme. But considering the key nature of this proposal, the Board was given extraordinarily little guidance as to how it was to behave, particularly in the matter of supervising how companies it assisted actually used the assistance they received. Any idea of public ownership was ruled out. The Report said, 'We have made our recommendations on the basis that there will be a high degree of co-operation on the part of the industry with the Board, and in these circumstances we are not recommending nationalisation or state participation as necessary to the improved competitiveness of the industry.'[5] In fact co-operation between the Board and industry was a long way short of perfect and the Board had few means of forcing its views on groups it had aided even if things were going badly wrong. It had no means even of ensuring that groups did what was necessary to keep to their own targets. The Expenditure Committee of the House of Commons in its report 'Public Money in the Private Sector' came to the conclusion 'The SIB regarded it as

5 Shipbuilding Inquiry Committee 1965-66 Report (HMSO) para. 333

within their power to change management as a condition of giving financial assistance, but once the money had been committed SIB were unwilling to put further pressure on management.'[6] In fact, lacking guidance from the Geddes Report, or powers in the Shipbuilding Industry Act, the Shipbuilding Industry Board adopted towards groups it had helped to form an attitude similar to that of the government towards Rolls Royce. The Board negotiated the assistance and then left the groups to get on with it until they came back for more.

Upper Clyde Shipbuilders came back for more again and again. The formation of this group was understood at the time to be highly risky and to be justified only on the grounds that the alternative was to allow the firms on the Upper Clyde to collapse individually. Any hope of the group's survival depended on constant supervision and pressure from above, neither of which was forthcoming. In the end the SIB simply handed the problem back to government, in despair no doubt at its own failure.

The government response has been to go back to square one; at the end of 1972 the Industrial Development Executive commissioned a major study by a well-known firm of American consultants to advise it on what to do.

The object of this unfriendly analysis of the Geddes Report is not to prove that it was a bad report. On the contrary it was in many ways a rather sensible report. Fed into a continuously learning administrative machine it would have done some good. It would have alerted officials to important aspects of the industry. It would have improved the government's performance as 'sponsor' of the industry. But it became a bible, a substitute for thought, a point of continuing reference when changed circumstances had made its recommendations much less relevant. In short, instead of an aid to learning, it became a block in the way of learning. The way to learn is to be involved in day-by-day administration. But the Civil Service did not want to be too deeply involved.

6 Expenditure Committee *Public Money in the Private Sector* (HMSO) (Session 1971-72) para. 104

The Geddes Report was a way out of involvement. It justified the government shuffling off much responsibility from its own shoulders to those of the Shipbuilding Industry Board. The Shipbuilding Industry Board was provided with quite inadequate guidance and was not capable of writing a sufficient remit for itself.

It is not proposed at this point to discuss in any depth the question whether, in this type of intervention in industry, it is better for the government to act directly or though a para-governmental agency. There is a strong argument where the considerations are as political as they are in the case of the shipbuilding industry, or where there is a strong likelihood that government will be involved in any case, that the government should act directly. On the other hand an agency is far more likely, if it is so motivated, to exert pressure to eradicate inefficiency than is a government. What is certain is that if there is to be an agency, it must be a continuing agency, working with a continuing responsibility for the use of the public money it allocates—a responsibility from which it cannot expect to be released by blissful death.

In this case the government fell, none too neatly, between two stools. On the one hand its agency was temporary and therefore, even if it had wished, could not have accepted a continuing responsibility for the public investment. On the other hand, the government, having tried and failed to retreat from day-to-day contact with a continuing and highly political problem, lost opportunities either to learn from experience or to bring to bear on the industry such pressure as governments can for greater efficiency. It would be wrong to blame the Geddes Committee for the failure of the policy it recommended, even though few committees have had so much of their advice accepted. The Geddes Committee did not have the handling of its own advice; if it had, it might have changed that advice in the light of experience. By no concept of ministerial responsibility can governments shuffle off to advisory committees the blame for their having adopted inelegant postures. It is the fault of governments if they accept the advice they have sought, or if they regard it not as enlightenment but as law.

Chapter 7

THE PROBLEM OF
MINISTERIAL RESPONSIBILITY

1. *Introduction*

The problem of responsibility is a central issue in industrial policy. Without responsibility there can be no accountability. Without responsibility there may be insufficient care in the preparation of action, which will therefore be the more likely to go awry.

Responsibility has always been regarded as a vital concept in government. Responsibility gives its own particular edge to decision-making. There are of course many constraints on decision-makers in government: dedication to the public interest, reputation, the prospect of promotion. All these can operate without there being identifiable responsibility for particular decisions, without there being any effective method by which responsibility can be brought home. It would be wrong to suggest that if the framework of responsibility is inadequate, the result will be irresponsibility. It is not with such an extreme that one is concerned. But if the framework of responsibility is inadequate, an ultimate discipline which has always been thought of particular value in the conduct of government is lacking.

It is easy for governments to spend public money in industry. Such expenditure will appear to be the solution to a great many problems, particularly political problems. It will satisfy those who insist that something be done without being quite clear what that should be. It will usually be popular, and may sometimes be wise. It has not always been the experience that it is as productive as it is popular.

When they spend money in industry, governments are frequently responding not simply to outside pressure but also to vested interests within government. These vested interests exist within departments and within government research laboratories. They may express themselves by ideas in the imperial tradition, such as the *British* aero-space idea or the *British* nuclear energy idea or more generally in the *British* technology idea. These ideas all have this in common: there has been little accountability, little attributable personal responsibility, and insufficient concern with the rate of return on expenditure however measured.

It is for these reasons that the problem of responsibility is so central to government–industry relations. But it is an intractable problem by the very nature of democratic government. The most savagely truthful and, for our purpose, relevant remark ever made about politics is this: a week in it is a long time.

The very fact that this is a truthful, far more than a cynical, remark pinpoints the problem that in politics the issue of responsibility may be deflected by time, new crises and, indeed, general reputation. Governments live by their general reputation rather than by particular successes or failures. No doubt particular successes and failures condition the general reputation. But just because the memory of individual failures may be absorbed into the general stream of consciousness, responsibility is blunted. Yet in the end the reputation of a system of government in this country depends on its achieving a record of success, not on its ability to distract attention from its failures. The fact of big government accentuates the problem of responsibility. If one accepts that big government is here to stay because governments are held to be accountable for far more than they used to be, then it is on the problem of responsibility that attention must be focused.

2. *Government and Society*

The concept of responsibility is, from the very start, blurred by the complexity of a government's relationship to its society. For much, for which it is held responsible in an electoral sense, it is not in fact exclusively responsible. Frequently it is not responsible to any significant degree at all. There are many fields of economic and industrial activity in

174 POLITICAL RESPONSIBILITY AND INDUSTRY

which at most it can exercise influence, sometimes a powerful influence, but sometimes only a very moderate influence. Yet if the level of investment is low or the rate of inflation is high, it will take the blame. Much of the most public, day-to-day, activities of government are an attempt to influence the general economic situation of the country by a process of consultation and even negotiation with other powerful factors in society, such as the trade unions and the leaders of industry. It is influence, not power, that a government is attempting to exert, and the results depend not just on itself but on the course of the negotiations and, indeed, on the ability of the leaders with whom it is talking to carry their followers with them. Today, the ability of anyone to talk on behalf of anyone else, to negotiate on behalf of anyone else, is highly conditional. Governments know when they conduct this type of discussion, whether it be at Number 10 Downing Street, at the National Economic Development Council or, at a lower level, in the separate departments of state, that while they may be using the best channels of influence that exist, it is no more than the best available substitute for that form of leadership which, in times of war or crisis, can still sometimes be exerted by speaking direct to the people; or which, in the not too far distant past, could be exerted by concluding firm, if informal, agreements with groups of men who could speak for and bind their followers.

Because these days fewer and fewer men of power, whether they be businessmen or trade union leaders, come into politics, politicians are of less substance as individuals and are more and more simply spokesmen of their party. The party battle is concerned to a lesser extent with individual responsibilities and to a greater extent with collective responsibility. Collective responsibility is a poor substitute, most of all where industrial policy is concerned. Ministers serve and they go. From dust to dust, the ministerial incarnation in between is miraculously accomplished by Prime Ministerial nomination authenticated by the mystery of a peck at the royal hand. But what the Lord has given the Lord can take away. How can one attach much responsibility to what may be, so imminently, a pile of backbench dust?

Whether individual governments survive at the polls will depend on their general reputation, the credibility of the alternative and, perhaps, to some degree, on the electorate's view of itself. In this sense, governments collectively are responsible to the electorate. But when one comes to examine the capacity of the system of government, rather than the reputation of individual governments, and particularly when one comes to consider the capacity of government to develop fruitful relations with industry, then one must consider the problem of responsibility as it manifests itself in the course of day-by-day decision-making.

The individual, or the individual company, is concerned with the individual decision and the possibility of attributing responsibility and ensuring accountability for that individual decision. The system of government must provide that possibility. Bad decisions can be made by good governments. It is little comfort to an individual interest group, or to an individual company, that the general record of a government is good if there is no effective appeal against what seems to them a bad decision in their individual case. If there has been any breach of law an appeal may lie to the Court. If there has been any administrative failure, it may be possible to secure redress through the Parliamentary Commissioner for Administration. But if it is just a bad decision, and administratively proper, the system should provide hope of redress. It should also ensure that in the taking of these individual decisions there is proper care and proper consideration supported by adequate study. Responsibility is the guarantee to the individual that his case will not be settled in a fit of absent-mindedness and that, if there is error, there will be compensation.

3. *The Minister*

The chief departmental decision-maker is the minister appointed by the Prime Minister. Unlike the American system in which, despite the existence of separate departments of state with their ministerial heads, all executive power and all responsibility is vested in the President, under the British system a minister is executive head of his department, he carries ministerial responsibility for his department, and the

Prime Minister, in theory if not in recent practice, is simply *primus inter pares*.

Ministers are temporary, and the time-scale of policy will probably be long. It is the more difficult to attribute responsibility due to the time-scale of appreciation, decision, implementation, feed-back and final outcome. There is a rather general rule that the man who will carry the can is not yet in his post. Many ministers upon whom it has fallen to negotiate with the French some further stage in the Concorde project, must have cursed the original progenitor—Julian Amery—watching progress with pride and complete lack of responsibility either from the opposition benches in the House of Commons, or, latterly, from an entirely different ministerial responsibility in the Foreign and Commonwealth Office. He started it. His estimate of cost has turned out to be a vulgar fraction of the eventual staggering commitment. But they, not he, have succumbed to the pressures to continue. It would not fall to him to pay the bill whether in money or in jobs lost if the project were cancelled or turned out to be less than a commercial success.[1] The time-scale of the Concorde project has, of course, been long even by governmental standards. But it is not untypical in government that the time between decision and completion is long, far longer, for example, than is normal in industries less dependent on government support than aerospace or nuclear energy.

Ministers are a great deal more temporary than chairmen of companies. Even if Prime Ministers do not move them, the electorate may. In thirteen years of Tory government between 1951 and 1964 there were six Chancellors of the Exchequer, five Presidents of the Board of Trade, ten Ministers of Defence. This is a very different situation from that before the war when many ministers could expect to be in post throughout a parliament. It is almost as though these days the key to political success is to arrange to be moved before the

[1] A. W. Benn, MP, speaking in the House of Commons on 11 December 1972, referred to his 'sense of awesome responsibility' in dealing with Concorde. It is difficult to see what responsibility Mr Benn, or any of the other ten to a dozen ministers who have succeeded Julian Amery up to this date really had for this project, other than for not cancelling it. (House of Commons *Official Report* vol. 848, col. 116)

attributable embarrassment begins. Does it ever occur to a minister as he takes his big decisions that when the chickens come home to roost, he himself will be roosting elsewhere? Whatever the merits or demerits of the Industrial Relations Act, Robert Carr was elsewhere when trouble began. The decisions for which a minister may be called effectively to account will be those that take immediate effect or have immediate impact. His common sense must tell him what these are, and his political antennae must tell him how they will be received. He must often be tempted to buy off trouble with decisions that will postpone accountability. But whether or not he is cast in the mould that postpones trouble rather than confronts it, inevitably for a great many of his major decisions he can never be called to account.

It has been argued in support of frequent ministerial changes that a minister who remains too long will become the prisoner of his department, that frequent changes bring to a department fresh political impetus and prevent the minister becoming just another civil servant.[2] It is not in fact easy to prove the beneficial consequences of frequently injecting this new political impetus into departments. But whatever can be said about that, there is no doubt that frequent changes lessen responsibility. Moreover it is not just ministers who are temporary. In this sense, civil servants with their frequent moves from post to post are temporary too.

Ministerial responsibility is shared with cabinet colleagues and with junior ministers in the same department. A cabinet minister who allows himself to be overborne by his cabinet colleagues as to what should be done in his own department, and yet remains in post, should not be permitted to claim that his personal responsibility for the consequences is thereby one whit diminished. The problem is more difficult when responsibility is delegated to junior ministers in a department. Ministers may be, and frequently are, reluctant to delegate. But in massive departments, such as the Department of Trade and Industry, there must be delegation if there

2 See, for example, Richard Crossman *Inside View: Three Lectures in Prime Ministerial Government* (Jonathan Cape, The Godkin Lectures 1970) p. 76

is to be any hope that the department will function at all.
Yet the ministerial head of the department must still retain
'overall' responsibility, he is still representative of his department in cabinet and its principal spokesman in Parliament.
His major political troubles may grow out of small beginnings.
It would be very difficult for him to escape blame unless the
head of his junior is large enough to be an acceptable prize
for his political opponents. Yet whatever may be arranged
in such circumstances by way of ritual sacrifice at the
appropriate hierarchical level, there is here once again considerable danger that, retrospectively, it will be impossible
to say who was responsible.

The problem of responsibility is not made easier when
there is, as is often the case in government–industry relations,
some difficulty in assessing the output from policy. Take for
example the case of Upper Clyde Shipbuilders. Many millions
of pounds were poured into the company after its formation
in 1968. It absorbed a high proportion of the financial
resources available to the Shipbuilding Industry Board for
the benefit of British shipbuilding generally. Every few
months it had to be rescued again. It seemed incapable not
merely of restoring its assets to profitability but even of
assessing from one month to the next what its cash flow
position was. By 1971 a receiver had been appointed and by
1972, with the assistance of further millions of public money,
its assets had been divided between Govan Shipbuilders and
Marathon. It is not easy to believe that, financially, the
future is any more promising than the past. Here surely one
can conclude that the lesson of hindsight is overwhelmingly
against the original decision to establish Upper Clyde Shipbuilders and confirms all the fears expressed at the time about
the wisdom of that particular Geddes merger.

But is there not in fact something to be put on the other
side? The decision of Mr Heath's government to pour vast
additional sums into shipbuilding on the Upper Clyde after
it had apparently decided not to, suggests that there may be
some benefit attributable to this cost. Instead of the catastrophic collapse of shipbuilding on the Upper Clyde that
would have taken place in 1968 and after, if public money

had not been injected under cover of the Geddes merger, there has been a rather slower run-down in employment in shipbuilding. More time has been given to absorb the redundant into other forms of employment. Instead of a confrontation with Scottish opinion which could have had costly economic consequences far outside shipbuilding, the process of contraction has been made politically manageable. It may be that in terms of social harmony, all those millions of pounds were worthwhile. But is there any way of measuring cost against benefit in a case like this? Is there any way of assessing how much harmony it is worth buying at how many millions? In cases like this the government must use its own judgment, and in its turn must be judged by those whose millions are spent. For those who say that government should not become involved in such matters, judgment is easy. For those who will say that if government does become involved the only criterion must be commercial success, judgment is fairly easy. But for anyone who sees in issues such as this a balance of considerations, social as well as economic, judgment, even retrospectively, is difficult. For such people, the cost-benefit calculation will be difficult to make, and so it will be more than usually difficult to know whether to attribute blame.

There is also the case of the computer industry which was saved in 1965 by an injection of public money but which is still a pensioner of the public purse. Was the 1965 decision right? From the point of view of ministerial responsibility, it no longer matters. Frank Cousins, the Minister of Technology who took that decision, resigned in 1966. Since then there have been at least three responsible ministers. They have taken, perhaps felt themselves with no choice but to take, the consequential decisions. But was that decision, which committed the British government to the support of a British industry which was obviously in a very difficult competitive situation and which would obviously have a very hard battle for survival, right? Many issues arise here other than commercial viability. How far does one want to be dependent on American technology? How far is it important for Britain to have a national source of computer hardware as well as a national source of computer software? And suppose national support is worthwhile at some cost, at what cost? Is there a maximum acceptable outlay? Is one not in fact entering upon as open-ended a commitment, once one starts on the road of support for the computer industry, as has proved to be the case in aerospace? Is it possible to give a clear answer to these questions which would make it possible, even retrospectively, to attribute blame for a decision taken in 1965, assuming it were worthwhile to do so?

There was the collapse of Rolls Royce. The company entered into a contract for the production of the RB211 engine. It was unable to fulfil the contract into which it had voluntarily entered, even with the help of unusually favourable launching aid from the government. In the end the Conservative government nationalised the aero-engine assets of the company and financed the completion of the engine. Who was responsible for the collapse? Certainly the directors of the company were responsible. They committed the company beyond what its resources could sustain. How far this error was venial cannot be said. But was the minister who responded so lavishly to their original appeal for help responsible? The cost to the public purse, particularly the unforeseen cost, has been very considerable. Was he responsible because he enabled Rolls Royce to think of entering into the contract in the first place, because in effect he took their advice as to their capacity to produce the engine without becoming liable for damaging penalties for delay or inadequate performance, because he failed to do what at the time nobody expected him to do—to exercise detailed financial and technical surveillance over the progress of a contract entered into by a company whose very name was synonymous with British technology, because he accepted the company's argument that without the RB211 engine their place in the world aero-engine league would be irreversibly prejudiced? Nevertheless if ministers can enter into launching aid contracts of this magnitude and yet escape responsibility, on however good or creditable grounds, what discipline is there to control the expenditure of public money?

It is ironical that the minister principally concerned should have been so blamed by the aerospace lobby for bringing about the collapse of Rolls Royce. One can imagine the reaction of that same aerospace lobby two years before if he had refused to assist Rolls Royce. That might have been the right decision but he would never have been forgiven for it, and as the subsequent history of the affair would thereby have been cut short no one would ever have known how right he had been.

Then what are the ultimate penalties of failure? For a civil servant, loss of promotion and in extreme cases dismissal. For a minister the defeat of ambition but, if he is a Conservative, the probability of a lucrative future. There is no shame in ministerial failure. There is thought to be too much luck in it all. It is rather like a parking fine. The minister who is judged to have failed may find himself in the midst of uproar while he remains, but once he has gone, perhaps to the City, perhaps to the Lords, perhaps just to the back benches of the House of Commons, he will easily establish himself as an honoured, though possibly frustrated, critic of his successors who will profess the highest respect for his judgment and experience. It may be all very painful for a man who feels a call to serve his country. But, very likely, for a conscientious minister or ex-minister, the principal sorrow will be to have let down his party and his government. For in the end the final allocation of praise or blame will be made by the electorate and that will be done on the record of the government generally, a record to which he may feel he has added a few unhappy pages. But precisely for that reason he will find that his colleagues—or erstwhile colleagues—in government will do their best to cover up for him in order to rescue themselves, as well as him, from the consequences of his error. And whether or not it is a comforting thought, retirement to the back benches will almost certainly end any furore. For in party political terms the purpose of ministerial responsibility is principally to attribute blame to a leading political opponent. If he is destroyed politically in the process, the object has been achieved. The Opposition will turn on his remaining front-bench colleagues. The fact that his failure may betoken something inadequate in the system of government, and not just—or perhaps not at all—in the man as an individual, is likely to escape notice in the excitement of the chase.

It may once have been satisfactory to rely for a final judgment on the general feelings of the electorate about the record of ministers collectively. When government was responsible only for providing a framework of law, for holding the ring, and perhaps for providing general incentives, the general feeling of the electorate may have sufficed as a check on their competence. But the more governments become involved in individual interventions, the more essential it is to ensure that responsibility is properly defined and that its attribution is not blocked by party politics. Governments are becoming increasingly involved in this type of selective intervention in industry. It is being done with less and less parliamentary control. Powers have long existed by which a government without any special parliamentary procedure can assist aerospace research and development and employment in development areas. Yet when the Conservative Government of 1963 helped to establish the Fort William Pulp and Paper Mill, they thought it right to ask Parliament, despite the fact that power existed under the Local Employment Act, to pass a special Act to authorise the public expenditure involved in view of the importance of the project. When Labour, by its Industrial Expansion Act, extended its power to assist production it at least provided that such industrial investment projects should require an affirmative vote of the House of Commons. The Conservative Government's Industry Act of 1972 originally provided for no parliamentary procedure at all before such schemes were implemented, despite the fact that it also provided more money for the purposes of selective intervention than ever before. However back-benchers of both parties united to insist that better provision for parliamentary control than the government originally intended should be written into the Bill.

Conservative back-benchers wanted it because they distrusted the whole philosophy of the Bill and wished Parliament to be a more effective restraint. Labour back-benchers, while not dissenting from the philosophy of the Bill, wanted greater parliamentary control as some means of ensuring that there was adequate thought before action, and that the powers under the Bill were not used for blatant electoral bribery without adequate opportunity for public criticism. The government conceded because it was more than usually sensitive to this type of criticism, the Bill itself being so great a departure from its own previous policies. The Bill was therefore amended to introduce additional forms of parliamentary control which the government had originally argued were unnecessary and perhaps undesirable; but even these forms of parliamentary control fell short of what was provided in the Industrial Expansion Act of 1968, and certainly far short of the previous Conservative policy in government and in opposition that each selective intervention of this kind should be authorised by a separate Act of Parliament. Thus while governments are becoming more occupied with the promotion of such schemes, Parliament is increasingly being removed from any form of control, ministers seem less and less compelled to justify their decisions, and responsibility is more difficult to enforce.

4. *The Minister in his Department*
The Civil Service is the efficient element in the constitutional system; and government is a relationship between the Civil Service and those who are their political masters for the time being. The ministerial head of each department is individually responsible to Parliament, and depends on his civil servants for advice and for the administration of his department. He cannot function without them. Their actions gain validity from his explicit or implicit sanction. His validity comes from no quality or power of his own but simply from his appointment by the Prime Minister and from his responsibility to Parliament.

The minister will find on appointment that he is at once equipped with the two closest and most considerate friends he has ever had, his permanent secretary and his principal private secretary. Both will be men of ability, one already a high-ranking civil servant, the other likely to become so. One is official head of the department, the other the minister's principal liaison with it. If the minister knows what he wants to do, they and their staff can do it, if it is humanly possible.

If he does not know what he wants to do, they and their staff will tell him. If what the minister wants to do appears to them unwise, they will warn him, they will point to other ways of approaching his object, they may even conspire to protect him from himself. But if he knows what he wants, is a determined man, and can carry his colleagues with him, he will get what he wants. If he does not know what he wants to do and turns to his civil servants for advice, they will from the moment he accepts it describe it as his policy and carry it out as such.

From the point of view of the location of responsibility, the minister–civil servant relationship is unique. It is a relationship which is difficult to describe, which needs to be experienced to be understood. It is difficult even to find analogies. Perhaps George I, arriving to be king of a country he did not know and whose language he did not speak, is the nearest. Ministers have to learn a new language very quickly, the language of government business. Perhaps another analogy is James I, believing himself to be a wise king, but in fact only saved from such follies as he did not commit by the experienced guardianship of the first Salisbury. The essential point is the outsider coming in, not just to be an insider, but be the top insider in his department; on first appointment not even having experience of the type of administrative machine that will be to his hand to use; looked to for guidance even while he himself is searching for enlightenment. Perhaps one can take the analogy of an outsider brought in to run a nationalised industry. But the complexity of the ministerial task is greater, the pitfalls both more obscure and more frequent. Lord Robens who writes scornfully of the many Ministers of Power with whom he had to deal, had himself the advantage of some months as deputy chairman of the National Coal Board before he had to take on the full load.[3] Such an opportunity for preparation is seldom given to a minister. The decision of the 1964 Labour Government not to devalue was evidently taken within forty-eight hours of their appointment by three men who had not been in office for thirteen years.

[3] Lord Robens *Ten Year Stint* (Cassell), *passim*

People who have worked their way to the top in business have not merely gained experience in the ways of the business world, they have measured themselves against their colleagues and subordinates. If they have insight they know the qualities of their staff, their strengths and weaknesses, and their strengths and weaknesses as compared with themselves. The minister has not measured himself against his civil servants, he has not found out their qualities for himself. His reaction to them may be modest or arrogant, too modest or too arrogant, very likely starting with arrogance and ending with modesty; starting with a political determination to override advice but ending with a willingness to study it both because it is easier to accept it and because he has learnt to respect, perhaps overmuch, those who have given it. It is not at all unusual for a minister to find that he does not measure intellectually against his senior civil servants, without being at all clear himself which qualities of his own are nevertheless an essential ingredient of the minister–civil servant mix if it is to function at its most fruitful. There is a danger of the minister psychologically resigning his judgment to theirs without their realising the extent of the trust he has deposited in them. They may be giving him the advice they think appropriate to the conduct of his policy, while he believes they are telling him what they themselves would recommend him to do if the decision were theirs. It is frequently alleged that ministers become captive to their civil servants when what may really have happened is that it is neither his policy nor theirs that is being conducted, but their idea of his policy. Such confusion of purpose in no way reduces his responsibility. But he may believe that in fact he is sharing his responsibility with them by taking their advice, while they believe they are simply supporting him in the discharge of his responsibility by providing him with an administrative structure for his policy.

Where there is a clear, well-established policy, a policy possibly embodied in statute, the problem of responsibility is easier to resolve. There can be delegation of effective responsibility and the minister simply has to make sure that he will be informed of the sensitive issues. But where policy is changing, either through the force of external circumstances or through a new political input, there is grave danger of confusion as to who is in fact taking the decisions and moulding the policy.

The theory of the system is magnificent. On the one hand a minister who has been elected and has a policy. On the other hand trained administrators who know how to carry policies into effect. On the one hand democratic responsibility, by its nature temporary; on the other hand a pool of governmental experience, ever added to, and by tradition permanent. On the one hand innovation, and on the other prudence. Flair married with skill, popular appeal with sound sense. But the reality is often very different.

The reality is different even with ministers who do have policies. It is very different with ministers who do not. Where a minister in an incoming government has a policy there will at any rate be some new political input, wise or unwise, into the department's work. As time passes, as ministers are increasingly absorbed into the system, policy will tend to be formed in the course of discussion between a minister and his department. A good minister can still enrich his department's work by his power of decision, his different insight, his political sensitivity. A poor minister will simply become a slave of his own department, nominally taking decisions which the department, in despair of getting any reaction from its minister, foists upon him. It is then that it emerges most clearly that ministerial responsibility can simply be a fiction necessitated by the existence of a permanent Civil Service within a democratic system of government.

A great deal is going on in a minister's department which is not innovative but routine and for which he is in no real sense responsible. Take, for example, time-scale. Public expenditure is committed many years ahead. Much of it cannot be changed. Much therefore of what is going on is the administration of expenditure sanctioned by his predecessors, even of different governments. A minister can gradually change the emphasis of expenditure. But unless he is prepared to see roads uncompleted, schools half built or previously agreed grants to industry not paid, he will have only limited influence over what may be the majority of his department's expenditure. Similarly his successors will inherit his decisions. His civil servants will be helping him to make new policy. But they will be spending a great deal of time taking the day-to-day decisions that arise out of the implementation of previous policy.

Departments have continuing routine functions. Many of them may not be known to the minister and certainly not influenced by him. In the James Tribunal Inquiry into the Vehicle & General affair it was estimated that well under one per cent of the work of the Department of Trade and Industry came to ministers.[4] The relationship between ministers and the department was there defined as follows:

> The ministers give political direction to the department's operations and pilot legislation through Parliament. Once the legislation has been passed and any ministerial guidance has been given, the civil servants are expected to take entire charge of the administration unless there are any problems about which they need guidance from higher up, or unless there are any matters of particular political sensitivity about which they think ministers would wish to know.[5]

Many of the matters which are not referred to ministers are of the highest importance, like the Vehicle & General affair itself. If ministers are questioned in Parliament about any aspect of their department's work, it will then be displayed before them. They will have an opportunity of influencing the way work is done. But as they will have been brought in at mid-point in a continuing policy, they may find that there is little that they can do in fact other than accept the departmental point of view and defend it. Usually they will be fortunate in that the work is being well done, and they may feel perfectly happy in accepting responsibility for it. But the responsibility is nominal, far more nominal for example than that of a board of a large company which takes

---

[4] Report of the tribunal appointed to inquire into certain issues in relation to the circumstances leading up to the cessation of trading by the Vehicle and General Insurance Company Limited (HMSO) p. 21 para 61
[5] ibid.

responsibility for the decisions, in detail unknown to them, of their subordinates. The board has probably had a continuing entity for a considerable period, the minister may have been in office for a relatively short period. Much that is done is simply the administration of existing law. Responsibilities falling on departments under the law of the land have to be discharged even if the law is, as it probably is, the product of earlier parliaments. Ministers may wish to change the law. But to change the law involves the consumption of scarce parliamentary time and of scarce departmental resources in the drafting of Bills. Other matters may have higher priority, and the department may therefore be left discharging functions that the minister thinks it should not discharge, or in a way in which he thinks unsuitable. Equally it may be left without powers that he believes it to need. In such cases it is difficult to know who is responsible for failures, the government for its choice of legislative priorities or Parliament for being a legislative bottleneck.

One example of the confusion about the location of responsibility is the appointment of departmental accounting officers. The accounting officers are those officials, normally permanent secretaries, who are legally responsible for departmental expenditure. It cannot be the minister because he may soon be gone. As enquiries of the Public Accounts Committee frequently take place years after the event, he probably has gone by the time he could be questioned. Therefore the accounting officers, not their ministers, answer to the PAC in the House of Commons. It is, of course, an answer to charges of unwise, or improper, expenditure, that they were instructed by their minister. If an accounting officer is in conflict with his minister on what constitutes proper expenditure within the departmental estimates, he can ask for written instructions. In practice that rarely happens. The accounting officer answers to the PAC for his departmental expenditure, and defends in reply to questions such aspects of the expenditure or the manner of administering it as are being challenged. One can find the anomaly that by the time expenditure is being questioned by the PAC, ministers have changed, and some of them have become members of the PAC. It is a rather odd aspect of our system of government that one may find an ex-minister, as a member of the PAC, questioning a civil servant about the administration of a policy for which the ex-minister was initially responsible and, perhaps, joining in presenting to Parliament a report stating that the administration was in some way defective. The reports of the PAC, however seriously regarded in departments, have the disadvantage of being politically anonymous. That is why ex-ministers can join, perhaps a little uncomfortably, in criticising themselves by implication. Yet the PAC could hardly criticise explicitly a minister or ex-minister whom it had not heard in his own defence; and even if it did hear him, such criticism would be regarded as an exercise in party politics rather than as a legitimate expression of its quasi-judicial function.

5. *The Myth of Ministerial Responsibility*

In these circumstances how stands ministerial responsibility? Ministerial responsibility is the ark of the covenant of the constitution. It cannot be right that this should be a form of responsibility which, on detailed examination of particular cases, is found to be unreal in that although where the decision was in fact the minister's, responsibility is frequently unenforceable; and that where responsibility is in fact delegated, a constitutional fiction still attributes it to him.

If one is looking at the realities rather than the constitutional fictions, there are three types of situation: where the responsibility of the minister is clear; where it is delegated unless there is reference to him; and where an important element of real ministerial responsibility remains even where there is delegation and no reference upwards. A relatively high proportion of industrial policy decisions will fall in the first or third categories.

(a) *Where the ministerial responsibility is clear.* These are the cases where the decision is the minister's or where it is unquestionably in fulfilment of his policy. These are the cases which fit most easily into the constitutional theory. The only difficulty is the fundamental one that responsibility will frequently be unenforceable against him either because there is no way of doing so, or because he is protected by the party system, or because he has left office before the results accrue. It may sometimes be possible to attribute blame retrospectively, but there are at least two difficulties. First it will seldom be possible to claim that there were no administrative options in the conduct of policy. The departed minister will almost always be able to argue that his policy would have been all right had it been conducted this way rather than that. The second difficulty is that the whole point of attributing responsibility is lost if it has to be attributed to a departed minister. The intention behind the concept of ministerial responsibility is to maintain standards in government and the reality of democratic control by a system of accountability to Parliament. In what form can a departed minister be held accountable, except perhaps by impeachment (an instrument of parliamentary control over the executive which has unfortunately fallen into disuse) or sometimes by an informed Press? In any case it could be too useful a method of escaping current responsibility if it could too easily be attributed retrospectively.

The only practical approach to this problem is to rely on the minister's sense of responsibility and on the checks and balances described in the next chapter; and to investigate how far decisions in implementation of an industrial policy can be hived off to a para-governmental agency with a continuing responsible existence.

(b) *Where responsibility is clearly delegated.* Civil servants can be and are held responsible for decisions which they take in the course of their duties.

The practical question is whether ministers, in delegating functions, thereby firmly locate responsibility and accountability to Parliament on those to whom those functions are delegated. Decisions of great importance are delegated to civil servants. There are the functions under the Companies and Insurance Companies Acts. There can be the lending of large sums of money to individual firms. Inevitably whatever ministerial guide-lines are laid down, large areas of discretion are left to civil servants. The creation of the post of Parliamentary Commissioner for Administration is some protection against administrative impropriety. But where judgment is being exercised in the pursuance of policy there is need for a clear and publicly known framework of responsibility. Sir Richard Clarke proposes that officials below the rank of accounting officer should be designated as responsible for specific areas of expenditure and be liable to summons as witnesses before the Public Accounts Committee to deal with such questions as might arise out of their work.[6] This would certainly be a step forward. In the end it might prove easier to enforce responsibility against civil servants than against their ministers in cases where delegation is clear.

(c) *Where real ministerial responsibility remains even if there is delegation.* Inevitably, delegation cannot eliminate ministerial responsibility. The more important decisions clearly involve ministerial responsibility even where they are not referred to ministers. There is an uncertain area in which both minister and civil servant may be liable to blame, but in which the real responsibility of the civil servant is greater than is that of the minister.

The most authoritative statement of the relationship between ministerial responsibility and civil servant responsibility is that given by Sir David Maxwell Fyfe, then Home Secretary, on 20 July 1954 in the course of the debate on the Crichel Down affair:

The position of the civil servant is that he is wholly and directly responsible to his Minister. It is worth stating again that he holds his office 'at pleasure' and can be dismissed at any time by the Minister; and that power is none the less real because it is seldom used. The only exception relates to a small number of senior posts, like Permanent Secretary, deputy secretary, and principal financial officer, where, since 1920, it has been necessary for the Minister to consult the Prime Minister, as he does on appointment.

I would like to put the different categories where different

6 Sir Richard Clarke *New Trends in Government* (HMSO) p. 12

considerations apply . . . where there is an explicit order by a Minister, the Minister must protect the civil servant who has carried out his order. Equally where the civil servant acts properly in accordance with the policy laid down by the Minister, the Minister must protect and defend him.

Thus the first two categories refer to the first situation described above where the responsibility of the minister is clear. Sir David then continued:

I come to the third category which is different . . . Where an official makes a mistake or causes some delay, but not on an important issue of policy and not where a claim to individual rights is seriously involved, the Minister acknowledges the mistake and he accepts the responsibility, although he is not personally involved. He states that he will take corrective action in the Department . . . he would not, in those circumstances, expose the official to public criticism . . . But when one comes to the fourth category, where action has been taken by a civil servant of which the Minister disapproves and has no prior knowledge and the conduct of the official is reprehensible, then there is no obligation on the part of the Minister to endorse what he believes to be wrong, or to defend what are clearly shown to be errors of his officers. The Minister is not bound to defend action of which he did not know, or of which he disapproves. But, of course he remains constitutionally responsible to Parliament for the fact that something has gone wrong, and he alone can tell Parliament what has occurred and render an account of his stewardship.

The fact that a Minister has to do that does not affect his power to control and discipline his staff. One could sum it it up by saying that it is part of a Minister's responsibility to Parliament to take necessary action to ensure efficiency and the proper discharge of the duties of his Department. On that, only the Minister can decide what it is right and just to do, and he alone can hear all sides, including the defence.[7]

7 House of Commons *Official Report* vol. 530 cols. 1286-7

It would be an exaggeration to suggest that these words are crystal clear. What does it mean to say that a minister is constitutionally responsible even if he did not know of an action and would have disapproved of it if he had? Reginald Maudling when Home Secretary attempted to help on this point in the course of the Vehicle & General debate on 1 May 1972:

> It is no minimising of responsibility of Ministers to Parliament to say that a Minister cannot be blamed for a mistake made if he did not make it himself and if he has not failed to ensure that that sort of mistake ought not to be made. In other words, this is where the blame of Ministers should arise. If a Minister gets it wrong or fails to ensure that the other chap has not got it wrong, that Minister is to blame. That does not stop Ministers being responsible to Parliament for what their Departments do.[8]

Presumably this means in practice that a minister is responsible to Parliament for ensuring that his department is working properly, and that his culpability will be judged by the importance of any error that occurs. Unfortunately difficulties remain. First, it is impractical for ministers personally to lay down guide-lines to cover the whole of their department's work, and they will therefore very frequently rely on senior officials to ensure that 'that sort of mistake' ought not to be made. Secondly, although Maudling was speaking in the Vehicle & General debate, his remarks on ministerial responsibility happen to be directly at odds with the findings of the James Tribunal.

The Vehicle & General Insurance Company Limited collapsed in March 1971. The circumstances of the collapse led to the establishment of a Tribunal of Enquiry under the Tribunals of Enquiry (Evidence) Act, 1921. Among the matters referred to the Tribunal of Enquiry was whether there was negligence or misconduct by persons in the service of the Crown directly or indirectly responsible for the discharge of functions under the Insurance Companies Act, 1958-67. These functions are functions of surveillance. The Tribunal

8 House of Commons *Official Report* vol. 836 col. 159

G

found that the under-secretary in charge of the Companies and Insurance Companies Division of the Department of Trade and Industry 'did not have, or did not exercise, the standard of competence in relation to the affairs of the company which was to be expected from him, and that his conduct in this aspect of his duties must be characterised as negligent under our terms of reference'. No minister was criticised by the Tribunal, although quite clearly, in Maudling's terms, ministers had failed to ensure against this sort of mistake. There was in this case a great deal more ministerial responsibility than the Tribunal allowed for, the difficulty being, as so often, to decide to which ministers or ex-ministers responsibility should be attributed in a case like this which continued over a period of ten years. There was, in particular, ministerial responsibility for the inadequacy of the system created to exercise the function of surveillance.

This function should long ago have been hived off to an expert public agency. It is a function with no political element justifying ministerial intervention. The functions of the Companies and Insurance Companies Division were regarded as so technical that civil servants were kept in post for much longer than normal. There is no reason at all to expect that most ministers will have the expertise to make informed judgments on the major questions that may be referred to them. Presumably this is the reason that such questions were so seldom referred even to more senior civil servants, let alone to ministers.

It makes nonsense of the whole concept of ministerial responsibility when it is used not to locate responsibility but to avoid responsibility being located at all—until there is a catastrophe and a Tribunal blames a civil servant for what were in fact the inadequacies of the system. Ministers can appropriately be held responsible for ensuring that there exists a control system which works. In a field such as this they should not be responsible for operating the controls. That means locating that responsibility somewhere, not in a department where there can be ambiguity as to the location of responsibility but in an expert public agency whose responsibility is clear and absolute.

The James Tribunal was probably wrong in failing to comment on the element of ministerial responsibility. But at any rate it was resisting the normal pressures which are to find overriding ministerial responsibility where there is any ministerial responsibility. There is first the party political pressure. Secondly, there is a sense of unfairness in blaming civil servants publicly when ministers so easily escape blame. Thirdly, there is the pressure that arises from the very nature of a permanent civil service. There should be public civil service responsibility and accountability. If there were, it might long since have been possible to hive off the function of company surveillance. But the fact of a permanent Civil Service makes such a concept difficult to establish, and ministerial responsibility becomes a convenient substitute even in the most inappropriate circumstances, thus merely serving to ensure that real responsibility is in fact nowhere located. Such a concept has been easier to establish in the United States of America where the top ranks of what we would regard as the Civil Service are subject to replacement by incoming presidents. As the occupants are temporary, and may be part of the political machine of the president, they can go if they are discomfited by what they have to do. Our Civil Service is permanent, it is loyal to all governments in turn, and its undoubted quality has been an essential element in maintaining standards of administrative integrity and competence in this country. It is more difficult to hold a man responsible for policies which are not his, of which he may as an individual disapprove, which he administers only because it is part of his job as a public servant, than to hold responsible a man who has come in as part of a political apparatus, who is therefore associated personally with its policies, who is not permanent or expected to be available to serve very different governments, and can therefore leave if he finds himself in disagreement with his masters. But it needs to be done.

This section is entitled 'the myth of ministerial responsibility'. Sometimes it is a myth because the minister is not in fact primarily responsible, if at all. Sometimes it is a myth because ministerial responsibility is not enforceable and therefore is not actually performing the function allocated to it under the constitution, the function of ensuring administrative integrity and accountability to Parliament. For administrative integrity we are relying on the devotion to duty of public servants of all kinds. We are dealing here with an area of policy in which the desire of government to maintain a good reputation with the electorate is not sufficient protection. Industrial policy involves a series of discretionary decisions, few of great public importance, in which there is discrimination between firms and in the course of which millions of pounds may be spent.

The framework of responsibility is not good enough for this purpose. It was partial recognition of this fact that led some departments in the past when they had to intervene to do so at arm's length, in the manner discussed in Chapter 6. At any rate real responsibility would then be located somewhere. But governments are being forced into ever more intimate connection with industrial problems. The establishment of the Industrial Development Executive, an agency[9] within the DTI, is a sign of this. But nothing in the constitution of IDE in any way meets the problem of responsibility discussed in this chapter. The statement by Sir Antony Part in the Appendix shows how the DTI is still trying to place responsibility at arm's length while accepting the necessity of deeper involvement by the department. The problem of the location of responsibility is increasingly likely to be confused rather than resolved.

In this chapter attention has been focused on the complexities of determining actual responsibility for what is done in a department; and on the protection which is given to a minister probably by the lapse of time, almost certainly by the facts of party politics, possibly by a general forgiving belief that the poor chap did not have much choice in the matter anyway.

It is because ministerial responsibility does not, in the case of industrial policy, provide the protection that constitu-

---

[9] Not too much significance should be attached to the term 'agency' which is apparently used to suggest that bodies like the IDE have to some extent an identity separate from the department. The IDE is in fact part of the department and is under its Permanent Secretary.

tionally it should provide, that it is so important to ensure that all major decisions of government in this field which involve discriminatory public expenditure are adequately explained and publicly justified at or near the time they are made. How far this objective is achieved is considered in the next chapter. Checks and balances of this kind should not have to be a substitute for responsibility, but a further protection. Yet if the framework of responsibility is inadequate, let us at least look to our checks and balances.

Chapter 8

OF CHECKS AND BALANCES

1. *Introduction*

Our forefathers long ago wisely decided that in addition to ministerial responsibility there should be some checks and balances. The theory of checks and balances assumes that power will be more carefully used when it has to explain itself and prove the need; that whatever sense of responsibility there may be in a minister to ensure that he sufficiently studies his problem before he makes his decision, that sense will be enhanced if he lies under the threat of having to account to others for his use of power. If a minister is up to his job, the checks and balances will be not a deterrent but a guarantee. If he is not up to his job, the checks and balances will keep him under some restraint until it is time for him to go. The existence of checks and balances assumes an authority independent of the government, set against the government. It assumes, in fact, some separation of powers. At the point at which Parliament took over executive power from the king, the most vital of all checks and balances, the threat of refusal of supply, began its rapid descent into complete disuse. Nothing equally effective, or even half as effective, has replaced it. Parliament, through an executive committee known as the Cabinet, exercises power. It has not yet devised any system by which it can also operate as an effective check on power.

2. *Parliament*

Parliamentary control of the Executive is particularly weak in the area with which we are here concerned, the making of decisions which in the course of implementing industrial policy discriminate between one company and another, one industry and another, one region and another. Parliament may indeed influence a government through its function of advising and warning where great issues of major political significance are concerned. But the day-by-day relations of government and industry are not of that kind. This is not to say that they are not important. They are very important to those immediately concerned. But they are not issues of such political moment that governments will tremble should Parliament frown. It is very unlikely that Parliament will frown. For Parliament is rather poor, inevitably so, in focusing on specific decisions of this kind.

One hundred years ago parliaments could and did overthrow governments. They could and sometimes did deny to governments the legislation those governments desired. Yet even then, as Bagehot wrote: 'It is perfectly possible—it has happened, and will happen again—that the Cabinet, being very powerful in the Commons, may inflict minor measures on the nation which the nation did not like, but which it did not understand enough to forbid.'[1] Bagehot therefore sees a value in the House of Lords which, he believes, can 'impede minor instances of parliamentary tyranny'.[2] It is precisely minor decisions, those which did not lead to the overthrow of governments even in Bagehot's time, with which in industrial policy we are repeatedly concerned. It would be nonsense to believe that, whatever was true one hundred years ago, the House of Lords could today act in such matters as the 'Tribunal of Revision', in such minor matters which Bagehot wanted. The House of Lords would not dare.[3] As we are here normally dealing with money matters, it has not now, even in theory, the power. Both the Industrial Expansion Act 1968 and the Industry Act 1972 confine such parliamentary control over government action in this field as they permit, to the House of Commons. It is the House of

[1] Walter Bagehot *The English Constitution* (The World's Classics) p. 96
[2] ibid. pp. 96-7
[3] Nevertheless in fairness it should be remembered that the House of Lords played an important role in securing the reversal of the Stansted—Third London Airport—decision.

Commons that is so inadequate a check on government in this field.

Parliament is far too large and too amorphous a body to be responsible for decisions. It is government that has power, that should have responsibility, that may be held responsible by the electorate at a general election. Parliament is therefore very disinclined, even if it had the power, to refuse a government what it, in its responsibility, wishes to do. It may ask it to explain. It may question critically, it may, through a select committee, report adversely. But it will seldom refuse if the government insists because it is the government that is responsible. It is because of Parliament's awareness that it cannot in the end withhold support from the type of day-by-day decision that a government takes in the course of its relationship with industry, that Parliament is in fact rather poor in equipping itself even to comment on such decisions. Yet, provided that the government is acting legally, Parliament is the only check there could be on the individual decisions of government. Others may advise but only Parliament could thwart.

Opportunities of course exist for interests affected by government decisions to consult with Members of Parliament. Industries may brief them. The Members of Parliament can then raise those issues in Parliament and the government may then be compelled to explain itself. But this process will not influence a government which is satisfied that it has correctly assessed the representations it has itself received in the wider context of the national interest, and which knows that it can rely in the end on the confidence of its own supporters. It is for this reason that so many powerful interest groups which may once have thought it important to have leading figures in Parliament, now think it much more important to have their own private access to government and to influence directly those government policies by which they may be affected. If they fail in those representations, they may then fall back on Parliament. But Parliament is very much a second best and is unlikely to undo by its influence, or by the influence of some few of its members, what the government in its majesty and responsibility has decided to do.

Thus the most that can be claimed for Parliament is that it has a right to ask ministers to explain, a right which is enacted in the Industry Act 1972 in that certain of the more important or more controversial decisions will have to come to it for approval. But this is an approval which Parliament is scarcely equipped to give and less equipped to withhold. If Parliament wished to do this job more effectively, the obvious method would be for the Public Accounts Committee to enquire into specific examples of government assistance to industry, in advance of a decision or immediately after. This is something we discuss in the next sub-section.

3. *Select Committees*

There has been in recent years an efflorescence of Select Committees. New Select Committees with particular relevance to our theme are the Expenditure Committee and the Select Committee on Science and Technology. These Select Committees have given some MPs and some journalists the illusion of greater parliamentary control over governments. They have certainly provided a far better opportunity than can Question Time in the House of Commons, to probe ministerial policies by detailed questioning. They have produced reports of varying quality; some may have influenced government; some may have contained useful evidence which compelled departments to think about policies too easily taken for granted.

Their role and their possibilities should not however be exaggerated. Richard Crossman, as Leader of the House of Commons and one of the prime movers in the creation of the new Select Committees, has said 'We thought in a minor way they might provide occupation for our frustrated backbenchers.'[4] The executive, he pointed out, has nothing to fear from them because 'the Whips control everything'.[5] Comparing Select Committees of the House of Commons with the model on which they supposedly were based, he said 'Just imagine a Senatorial Committee in which the President could order, through the Whips, the removal of any member of the

4 Crossman, op. cit., p. 102
5 ibid. p. 103

Committee who had been awkward.'[6] In any case, any Member of Parliament would rather be a Parliamentary Secretary than a member of a Select Committee. For effective parliamentary Select Committees one needs either constitutional separation of powers or, at least, a House of Commons more independent of government than is ours today.

Thus the first point to be made about Select Committees as a check on the government is that made by Crossman, that the Party system is overriding. One would not expect them within the British parliamentary system, as it now exists, to be a threat to government policy. They will not even act very satisfactorily as a check.

The second point, sometimes overlooked by indignant members of Select Committees whose recommendations have been ignored, is that they cannot any more than the House of Commons itself, take responsibility for decisions. The purpose of Select Committees is to exercise a check on government by satisfying themselves that the proposals of the government are or were likely to achieve the government's stated objective. Making their own recommendations is a secondary activity into which Select Committees can be too easily diverted and which may frustrate their prime function of acting as a check on government.

Labour Members of the 1967 Select Committee on Science and Technology now take understandable pleasure in the Conservative Government's 1972 announcement that the development and sale of nuclear power plant should be concentrated in one organisation instead of having two competing consortia. This is in line with what the Select Committee then recommended but which was rejected by the Labour Government of the time. But if government believes itself right and the Select Committee wrong, how can it possibly defer to the view of the Select Committee? Select Committees have a right to recommend, to advise, to warn, to criticise, all the rights of the House of Commons itself. They have no right to decide because they cannot take responsibility. It may sometimes happen that a Select Committee is right and the government

6 Crossman, op. cit., p. 103

wrong. That possibility justifies a government in taking seriously what a Select Committee recommends. But a government cannot possibly surrender its judgment to the judgment of a Select Committee. Indeed, no government should have the right to claim later in its own defence that it simply followed the recommendations of a Select Committee. Governments must act on their own judgment in the light of their own responsibilities. The view of a Select Committee can serve to confirm a government's decision; it can perhaps lead a government to think again. But a government cannot share its responsibility with a Select Committee. If it could, one would have to say that the existence of Select Committees was simply making a bad situation, with inadequate ministerial responsibility, worse not better. It would further confuse responsibility.

The further difficulty about Select Committees as a check on government arises from their speed of action. Governments do not invariably act quickly, but no government could conceivably allow the timing of its decisions to be dependent on the concurrence of a Select Committee meeting possibly for a couple of hours once a week during the parliamentary session.

The only Select Committee that to some extent breaks through these limitations is the Public Accounts Committee. The Public Accounts Committee has the advantage of the advice and guidance of the Comptroller and Auditor General and of the Exchequer and Audit Department. The Public Accounts Committee could probably re-organise its priorities in order to take a severe look at government decisions to invest in industry nearer the time at which they were being made. It would call ministers and not just accounting officers. This might require some change in its terms of reference. The Public Accounts Committee needs also to extend its remit from the supervision of candle-ends, some of them no doubt rather large candle-ends, to a critical examination of the methods actually being adopted to achieve each department's objectives. The present division between the Expenditure Committee and the PAC should be redefined. The PAC should combine the Expenditure Committee's current but neglected responsibilities for ensuring how policies could be carried out more economically, with its present task of supervising actual expenditure retrospectively. With additional resources and working in sub-committees with the aid of the Comptroller and Auditor General and the Exchequer and Audit Department, the PAC should do a thorough job of investigation and report on the implementation of government policy from its inception. This would not mean that the Public Accounts Committee was taking responsibility for any action of government. It could not authorise action and it could not subsequently provide an excuse for decisions made. The government must stand on its own feet. But the Public Accounts Committee could compel a government to explain itself at a time when it would have to propound reasons for expecting success, not excuses for having compounded failure.

Select Committees, particularly a Select Committee such as the Public Accounts Committee, can be an effective means of forcing the government to explain itself. That would provide some check. A government might even change its mind! But only in the rarest cases could the House of Commons, acting on the advice of a Select Committee, say no to a firm government proposal for action.

4. *The Civil Service*

Another check on government can be provided by the Civil Service. Moreover it is a check that has the welcome characteristic of privacy. The Civil Service gives its advice in private. A wise minister supported by capable civil servants is more likely to escape the unwelcome publicity which ill-thought-out schemes might arouse. The minister, in seeking the advice of his civil servants, will explain what it is he has in mind and why he thinks it will achieve his objective. That process will lead to the abandonment of some ideas and the improvement of others. If the minister is competent, it will be the bad ideas that are abandoned and the good ones that are improved.

As a check on ministers, the Civil Service inevitably suffers from certain defects. The first and fundamental defect is that it is under the control of ministers. It takes orders. It may advise and warn. It cannot rebel. The fact therefore that a minister comes forward with a project does not mean that it has the approval of his civil servants. It may have. When looking at some ministers, one may hope that it has. But if it has not, he is just as entitled to bring it forward and they, as his devoted slaves, must implement it as best they can. A second defect is that departments themselves have vested interests. They are not impartial judges of the national interest. They themselves have a point of view and a staff to protect. It will take a strong minister to fight successfully against his own department's vested interests. Indeed they may put it to him that if he does not fight for them, they will have no spokesman in Cabinet, that therefore he must speak for them, if not from conviction, at least so that the balance is held aright. Having the ear of the minister, having their hands on the public purse, makes these vested interests particularly powerful. One could be a great deal happier about the deficiency in attributable responsibility if one could be more certain of the impartiality of the government machine. Whether as cause or effect, if one looks at the white-hot elephants that have trumpeted on the British technological scene since the war, they all have, or have had, friends very close to government.

The Treasury is intended to be part of the nation's protective apparatus against the excesses of departmental vested interests. Mr L. Pliatzky of the Treasury, in evidence to the Expenditure Committee, spoke of the Treasury's role as being 'to bring our professional scepticism, so to speak, to bear on all the estimates and we are very seldom wrong when we do that.'[7] The Expenditure Committee commented that they 'feel some scepticism of our own about [the Treasury's] success'.[8] The Treasury like other departments is a servant of each successive government. It is no part of the Treasury's function to frustrate the will of ministers. The Treasury may be sceptical as to how far the proposals they are considering

[7] Expenditure Committee *Public Money in the Private Sector* (HMSO Session 1971-72) Minutes of Evidence p. 70 Q. 236
[8] Expenditure Committee *Public Money in the Private Sector* (HMSO Session 1971-72) para. 268

are the will of ministers and how far they are the will of spending departments expressed through ministers. But if ministers collectively decide to launch themselves on expensive technological projects, the Treasury's role is to obey. At that point in the process of decision-making there is no particular reason why ministers should have more regard to the Treasury's scepticism than to their own. The Treasury is not alone in scepticism. It has indeed repeated experience of cost escalation at the frontiers of knowledge. But this experience is not secret to the Treasury. Ministers who today embark themselves—or more properly the country—on such adventures do so in the light of an accumulated national experience of cost escalation and project cancellation.

Moreover the Treasury is not a technical department. It consists, certainly, of very able men. But there is nobody in the Treasury equipped to argue against a department that one technological project rather than another is more or less likely to succeed, more or less likely to overrun its estimates. Nor does the Treasury have more than the native capacity of its officials to lead it to insist against the responsible department that one form of public expenditure rather than another will lead to fulfilment of that department's objectives, whether they be reducing regional unemployment, rescuing a lame duck, staffing schools in educationally deprived areas or raising health standards in the nation as a whole. No doubt there would be even less control without the professional scepticism of the Treasury. To that extent the Treasury's role in public expenditure is as important in reviewing the detail as in controlling the total. But if the spending department itself does not provide an adequate check, the Treasury will not be able to fill the gap.

The major decisions of departments such as DTI and the Ministry of Agriculture, Fisheries and Food, departments which inevitably have intimate contacts with industry, should always be taken under the check of close interdepartmental supervision. The formation of large departments such as DTI has the effect of eliminating much of the interdepartmental consultation that was inherent in the more fragmented departmental system that preceded it. This may have advantages but it redoubles the importance of the supervision the Treasury, or a unit such as the Central Policy Review Staff, should exercise, without either body necessarily being particularly well equipped for the task. The single department, influenced by its close relationship with its sponsored industries, may prove a weaker negotiator on behalf of the national interest than it should be. If there is not proper supervision, national interests may go by default.

An important recent example of the dangers of leaving major decisions to single departments has arisen in the case of North Sea Oil and Gas. In 1971 a decision was taken to launch a fourth round of allocations of segments of the UK continental shelf. By far the greater part of these allocations were to be made (as had been the whole of the allocations in the three previous rounds since 1964) by ministerial discretion to applicant companies. There was no interdepartmental policy review before this fourth round even though it was the first since the discovery of oil in the North Sea in 1969. The only consultation was with the Treasury about the financial terms. These were left unaltered from the previous round. The discretionary allocations in this round, as in all previous rounds, were to be made against relatively nominal rents and a royalty of $12\frac{1}{2}$ per cent of well-head value was to be payable on commercial production from a successful find. It was later admitted that the financial terms could have been hardened. There was no interdepartmental consultation on the area of continental shelf to be allocated. DTI considered it necessary to have a large round in order to maintain the 'momentum' of work in the North Sea which was falling off. It was later admitted that the round had been too large even for that purpose, but by the time of that admission valuable properties in the North Sea had been allocated for periods of over forty years on financial terms too favourable to the oil companies.

DTI decided as part of this round, and in order to gain experience, to try a small auction experiment. Tenders were invited for fifteen blocks in the North Sea. The tenders were to be in the form of premia offered for these blocks over and above the normal nominal rents. These fifteen blocks were a very small proportion of the total allocation made during the round. The tenders were opened before the discretionary allocation actually took place. To the surprise of DTI, it was found that a total of about £135 million had been offered by way of premia for the fifteen blocks. The successful tenders amounted to £37 million. At this point it became obvious, if it had not been so before, that the terms on which the discretionary allocation was to take place were very favourable to the companies and unfavourable to the Exchequer. Yet DTI continued with the discretionary allocation with unaltered terms because it claimed that public faith had been pledged. There was no legal compulsion on the government to take that view. The whole question of the financial terms could have been reopened. But it was not. The discretionary allocation went ahead at great cost to the Exchequer. This was a decision of DTI alone. There was no consultation even with the Treasury. DTI ministers were told of the result of the tender but did not even raise the question as to whether the financial terms should be changed in the light of the enormous sums offered in the tender. A decision costing this country millions of pounds was taken by a single department by a process of unconsidered drift. It was a major failure of the machinery of government. It emphasises the importance of adequate interdepartmental machinery.[9]

Ministers are today less likely to get a monolithic view from their officials. They are far more likely to get a variety of options canvassed in memoranda and argued in front of them. The probability that this will happen both in departments and in Cabinets has, no doubt, been enhanced by the existence of the Central Policy Review Staff in the Cabinet Office (under, at present, Lord Rothschild).

However the area in which departmental views may still be monolithic is that in which the prospect of high cost and of cost escalation is greatest, the area of advanced technology. It would be interesting, for example, to know whether anyone in the Ministry of Technology gave Anthony Wedgwood Benn advice to the effect that the RB211 was not essential to

[9] First Report of the Committee of Public Accounts, Session 1972-73, North Sea Oil and Gas.

Rolls Royce's future in the major aero-engine business. Mr Ian Morrow now disputes Rolls Royce's claim at that time that if they had not gone ahead with the RB211 the firm would very rapidly have run downhill to the point where it would hardly have been viable.[10] Where a country has only one aero-engine manufacturer, or only one design authority for nuclear energy, the danger that all advice will be to the same effect and will indeed be merely a repetition of advice originating from an interested party, is greatly enhanced. Of course, if a minister does get competing advice, that provides no assurance that he will choose wisely. The choice will indeed be immensely difficult, not merely technically but politically, because one can be sure that the full fury of the lobbies will be let loose. But awareness of the existence of other options can be of value in probing proposals. If, for example, advice had been available that Rolls Royce could continue perfectly satisfactorily without the RB211, the inclination to investigate the proposal more deeply, to insist on tougher negotiation of the contract, would have been greater. If the choice was simply the RB211 or slow decline, critical faculties may have tended to go to sleep.

Another circumstance in which ministers may still be confronted with monolithic advice—or what amounts to the same thing, a variety of options among which one is obviously the preferred—is where they feel themselves confronted with a crisis and that rapid action seems essential to deal with it. It would appear that round about December 1971, ministers became seriously alarmed that unemployment was not responding as had been expected to the Chancellor of the Exchequer's reflationary policies. As the problem had not been thought about, as the government had been content to rely up to that point on market forces and macro-economic stimuli, there was nothing for it—if a package of proposals was to be brought forward—but to assemble once again the different elements of the Labour Government's discarded regional policies and to present them in a new guise. This was the birth of the Industry Act 1972. It appeared that the real

10 Expenditure Committee *Public Money in the Private Sector* (HMSO Session 1971-72) para. 66

question in the minds of ministers was not what should be done, but how what had to be done could be so presented that it was in some respects at least arguably different from what the Labour Government had done. In circumstances such as this, ministers are not presented with real options. They are not presented with an analysis of the problem out of which policy grows. They are presented instead with policies which it is known can be administered because they have been administered before, and which seem to have some relationship to the problem which has to be tackled. After all, if a government faces the problem of regional unemployment, if in any case it wishes to reflate, then the expenditure of large sums of money somewhere in the neighbourhood of the problem is a politically acceptable way of handling the situation.

It is thus the case that although departments, especially the new large departments, may be less monolithic in the advice they give ministers than once they were, yet in a number of very important areas they are still monolithic. There is in this country an insufficiency of expert sources of competing advice. A permanent Civil Service is inevitably monolithic in that it alone has experience of actually administering the government machine, it alone can therefore decide what is or is not administratively practical. Even therefore where there are outside experts on the problem who have new proposals to make, those proposals have to be absorbed through the existing machine. If the Civil Service advises ministers that the proposals are impractical, it is very difficult for a minister to gainsay them. If the argument is simply that the new proposals do not meet the case for reasons known to the department but unknown to the outside authority, the minister can perhaps use his own judgment for there is no reason why he should not know the allegedly unsurmountable objections. But the argument from administrative practicability is a peculiarly compelling one, particularly to ministers who do not themselves have the experience of running large organisations.

Nevertheless, though with these important limitations, departments do act as a check on government expenditure in industry. That the Civil Service has an influence on government is a subject of frequent comment. It is perhaps surprising that departed governments should so often find it an excuse for their failures that they fell under the bondage of their civil servants. Yet it is true that to rely, to the extent we do, on departments to provide their own checks on themselves is, given the existence of departmental vested interests, to rely on an odd combination of reluctance to change with willingness to spend, the Civil Service's strange form of conservatism.

5. *Learning*

Reliance on the government machine to provide its own in-built check on government means, among other things, relying on the capacity of the government machine to learn from experience.

Any democratic system diminishes the learning curve of government. That is part of the price we pay for democracy. It is not actually a high price because although experience is important, so are drive and freshness of approach. Queen Victoria was said to be more experienced than any of her ministers. But we may nevertheless be grateful that it was Gladstone who was Prime Minister, not Victoria. It sometimes happens that the best argument for re-electing a government is that, having had time to learn from its initial follies, it will probably be prepared to act sensibly in the future. This is a tired view of politics, for the sense of an old government may well be a sense of complacency and conservatism when what is needed is sensible new ideas. In politics, gratitude should never be anything other than a lively sense of favours yet to come.

Accepting that there is a loss of experience in the election of a new government, it is nevertheless reasonable to ask whether the system operates to keep that loss at a minimum or whether we are fated to see governments repeating the errors of their predecessors. The continuously learning element in our system of government is the Civil Service. They are the permanent servants of the Queen's government of whatever party and of whatever individuals it may consist.

Ministers bring in only a minimum of outsiders to assist them. The Civil Service cherishes its role as advisers to ministers and as it also controls the actual machinery of government its monopoly power is considerable. In return for that power it offers ministers the fruits of its continuous experience. How far ministers are guided by the advice they receive is a matter for them. After a time they will usually fall into the habit of being guided by it. It is only at the beginning of a period of office that a new government, imbued by ideas formulated out of office and conceived usually as dramatic solutions to prevailing problems, may curtly overrule the advice they receive. There is an eighteen months' learning period for new governments at the end of which time their initial political impetus is exhausted and they tend to return to consensus ways. Apart from anything else, accepting advice is both safer and simpler: safer because it is unlikely to be radical and because it comes from men who are more likely to feel committed to getting a minister out of a mess if they have got him into it—unless they decide that the mess is too bad and the minister must become expendable: simpler because it consumes less intellectual energy in the busy and exhausting life of a minister.

The return to consensus is therefore a standard feature of governments that begin by departing from it. Governments are rapidly exhausted by their initial experiments, and if these are not sensible and productive then the consensus to which they return is not even an enriched consensus. Or it is enriched only by the experience the Civil Service has fed into it rather than by the thinking of a new government. In the Industry Act 1972, it is impossible unfortunately to see any desirable new element that has been added to the hotchpotch of regurgitated industrial policy by Conservative thinking. The Industry Act does contain administrative improvements as compared, for example, with the Labour Government's investment grant system. But these improvements are certainly a Civil Service input, not a political input.

Something needs to be done to enrich the political input into government. To that end it is important to increase the policy-making capacity of oppositions. The availability of much more money would greatly help. Political parties are not at present able to prepare themselves adequately for government because they have not the resources to undertake the necessary research. Something more might be achieved if there were less secrecy in government. But the key gap is access to the Civil Service. If the Civil Service is to be permanent then its services should be permanently available, to Opposition as well as to government. It should be able to advise oppositions as well as government. It should be able to comment on policy statements prepared by the Opposition at the request of the Opposition. The Civil Service alone runs and knows how to run the machinery of the government. It alone has continuous experience of the operation of government. Preparation of policies without the assistance of the Civil Service robs a great deal of work of a great deal of its value. Incidentally, it also inhibits political debate as there is always natural scepticism of the practicability of Opposition programmes. This scepticism might be reduced if an Opposition was seen to be making sensible use of its Civil Service facilities. The mechanism for providing the Opposition with access to the Civil Service is a matter for debate. There would be need for great care if the Civil Service was not to be drawn into political controversy. One idea is the constitution of a Department of the Opposition staffed by civil servants on secondment from the different departments of government. This might not be the most satisfactory machinery as it might take able men out of the main stream of administration. It would be better to start such a radical departure modestly. Regular discussions between shadow ministers and senior civil servants might be a good beginning.

It may be thought that a consequence of such a proposal would be to make government in this country even more conservative and even more tied to the Civil Service than it is. This fear is probably not justified. What makes for conservatism in government is a series of new governments coming into office without practicable new ideas. Anything that enhances not just the generation of new ideas but the chance of their practical realisation would make government in this country more progressive, not more conservative.

Governments should do a great deal more to develop the idea of bringing into departments, and into a minister's office, persons of experience and ability whose political sympathies lie with the government and who have probably helped with the formulation of party policy. The burden on the minister is very great and he needs more help than he gets, particularly with the alleged administrative impediments to his policy. Able people sharing his political outlook, but perhaps of different background and experience, could provide that help. The principal difficulty is not the jealousy of the Civil Service but the tendency of ministers to come to rely far more on the advice of their civil servants than of their outside advisers. As a result, the outside advisers quickly pack up and go unless they are among the few who are listened to or they happen to enjoy their seat behind the minister at the political high table.

6. *A Para-Governmental Agency?*[11]

I have argued that in the area of industrial policy, ministerial responsibility is an insufficient guarantee and that we are dependent on a combination of partial checks for what is still a quite insufficient discipline on governments which spend public money in industry. The nature of our parliamentary system of government makes it difficult to suggest other than minor reforms in the control system.

Yet there can be no doubt that governments will continue to intervene in industry, and they may do so on a scale larger than they have in the past. The legislative authority for so doing now resides in the Industry Act 1972, the most far-reaching legislation ever enacted on this subject in this country. We have here what appears to be an insoluble conundrum. Governments will spend, yet there will be too little responsibility for what is spent, or how it is spent, and too little control through Parliament over the initial decision to spend. The question therefore arises whether any part of a government's interventionist activities can be hived off to a para-governmental agency.

[11] A valuable discussion of this question appears in the Expenditure Committee Report *Public Money in the Private Sector* chaps. 7-9

It is certainly the case that much of the task of intervention will still have to be discharged by DTI directly, particularly those tasks concerned with aerospace. In aerospace, government alone can decide whether to involve itself because the cost-benefit analysis is of a kind only government can make. The benefits can be summarised as national prestige, the avoidance of American monopoly, and employment for a large number of persons who have been trained in the work of the industry, who could find no comparable employment elsewhere, and some of whom might emigrate if there were no projects for them to work on. The costs are high and usually unknown in advance. The valuation of these benefits against such costs is a task for government. Similarly it would be right, at any rate in the early stages of such an agency, to leave government with the routine of regional policy, and possibly also with the more socially motivated rescue operations. A project like the aluminium smelters would still have had to be handled by government. It is clear therefore that governments will need to have a capacity for such action and it might be thought that that necessity is sufficient reason for abandoning any idea of having a para-governmental agency in addition. If governments sometimes need to intervene, should not all intervention be left to the direct responsibility of government? Yet the fact that government must have its own capacity to act should not exclude the possibility of creating such an agency to work in circumstances where the task is sufficiently definable in advance.

Such an agency would have to have terms of reference. They would restrict the agency to forms of intervention which in its judgment were to the economic advantage of the country. Its job would be to promote rather than to rescue.

One could start by allocating to the agency the majority of functions under Sections 7 and 8 of the Industry Act 1972. Section 7 deals with selective assistance in development areas. Section 8 deals with selective assistance in the country generally. Sometimes such selective assistance is required to rescue a bankrupt company. That would be a task for the agency where it judged the prognosis favourable. The government might act directly if the agency refused and yet the

216 POLITICAL RESPONSIBILITY AND INDUSTRY

government saw strong social reasons for action. The fact
that it was the government that was acting rather than the
agency would then have its own clear significance. Normally
the agency would not be concerned with rescues but with
tasks such as promoting new employment opportunities,
helping to develop business enterprises, accepting risks which
seemed reasonable but which had been refused by the market,
in other words with the broad spectrum of activities authorised
by Sections 7 and 8. The advantages of allocating such tasks
to an agency are likely to be greater commercial and industrial
expertise, speed and flexibility, combined with a clearer line
of attributable responsibility.

The agency would be answerable to the government and
to the Public Accounts Committee for its results. As it would
be answerable, it would be required that in any particular
case it should be satisfied that it could exercise adequate
continuing control over its investments. Its methods would
vary and would be for it to decide. Sometimes it might simply
act as an investment bank. At other times it might involve
itself in management. But whatever the method, it would
be responsible.

Sir Richard Clarke, with his great authority and experience,
says this:

My conclusion, therefore, is that the allocation of new tasks
to public Boards and Agencies is not necessarily wise, and
is positively dangerous if adopted for long term tasks; and
in my opinion we have to pay much more attention to our
capability within the public service to carry out these new
current tasks. I think it is right to set up public corporations
to do great permanent tasks.[12]

He has two main reasons for this view. The first is a fear
of atrophy in a small public board with a single task and a
small staff. Atrophy may set in because the staff has few
prospects and little outlet for its creative energies. The second
reason derives from a belief that departments have a duty
to equip themselves with the expertise to perform the functions, particularly the long-term functions, which ministers

[12] Clarke, op. cit., p. 89

impose upon them. If necessary, departments can seek the assistance of an advisory committee.

To a certain extent departments can equip themselves with full-time expertise, though perhaps not always at the highest level of ability. They can always command the services of an advisory committee, though such a committee, whatever its other excellences, can have the danger that it offers ministers a couch on which they can lay down their responsibility without its having any way of taking the responsibility upon itself. What departments find difficult to do is to rid themselves of inbred Civil Service attitudes born of protectiveness towards ministers and the public service; or to establish a system of attributable and enforceable responsibility. From the point of view of responsibility, an agency would have certain advantages. As a body with a continuing responsible existence it could carry responsibility for its results to an extent which governments never do. Thus at any rate in some part of the area of intervention there would be clearly attributable responsibility. Moreover the existence of such an agency would give a special select character to those acts of intervention which a government decided to perform for itself. Its existence would compel a government to say why they were taking the initiative rather than leaving it to their para-governmental agency with its more restricted terms of reference. This in itself would provide some degree of control over government intervention.

Something of this is provided in the Industry Act 1972 by the requirement that where there is disagreement between the government and the Industrial Development Advisory Board, a report has to be laid before Parliament. But the Industrial Development Advisory Board does not carry responsibility for what the government does. Parliament has provided no terms of reference to guide the advice it gives. As such parliamentary significance has been given to its dissent, it is likely to disagree publicly with the government only in extreme cases. A decision by a para-governmental agency not to take responsibility itself for a particular proposed intervention would be a far better warning signal and possibly more frequent. The Industrial Development Advisory Board is likely to turn out to be a hostage to the government's fortunes. It is in fact neither one thing nor the other. Neither independent nor governmental, neither responsible nor purely advisory. It has a kind of veto which may turn out to be as suicidal in use as the bee's sting. If it dissents, it creates a crisis which the government may have to resolve by using its parliamentary majority. If it does not dissent, then it shares the responsibility that the government should have to shoulder alone. It is a further confusion in the lines of responsibility. It is one of those devices that sap confidence in government because it saps the responsibility of government.

As relations of the State and industry do represent a great permanent task, perhaps the proposal that there should be an agency to discharge as much of that task as possible is not inconsistent with Sir Richard Clarke's view. Such an agency might in certain respects be comparable to those great public corporations, the nationalised industries. It may be held that the record of the nationalised industries is not in every respect admirable. Nor is that of private industry. Nor, more relevantly, is that of those departments of government which for many years now have been regularly investing in industrial activities. It would be difficult to claim that the record of any nationalised industry compared unfavourably with that of that massive investor of public money, the Ministry of Aviation in its various incarnations.

This type of agency would be of a different kind and would have an entirely different scope from the agencies increasingly running quasi-commercial activities in Whitehall. It would be performing in an area where there would be a very high degree of discretion in the development of its activities and it would be entirely outgoing, not founded on various requirements of the government machine itself, as are, for example, the Stationery Office, the Royal Dockyards, and ordnance factories. The point which it would have in common with these other agencies would be accountable management.

There are two arguments of principle that remain to be considered. However its remit was drawn, a para-governmental agency would have considerable discretion. It would discriminate between companies and might well appear to be discriminating between regions. If there is to be such discrimination, should not the instrument of it be a government department responsible directly to Parliament? This argument would be stronger if the departmental framework of responsibility within government and to Parliament was stronger. In fact the real accountability of a para-governmental agency is likely to be greater than the theoretical accountability of ministers. The agency here conceived would have a close statutory relationship to government and to Parliament and would be answerable to the PAC. It would however have an essential element of independence in that it would refuse to take on tasks, particularly tasks involving the expenditure of its own money where it felt unable to accept responsibility, just as it would itself be able to initiate action where it *was* prepared to take responsibility. The existence of the agency would itself pinpoint in a very special way the responsibility of government for its own selective interventions.

The second question of principle is whether it is acceptable that such an agency should have a power of deciding for itself on the expenditure of public money, a power which governments reserve to themselves because of their responsibility for the allocation of national resources between different priorities. The answer to this is that governments must indeed retain that power. But if they are prepared to spend a sum of money each year on selective assistance outside the advanced technologies, there is no reason why the agency should not be given an entitlement to such share of those resources as it felt able to spend, and answer for, in the national interest. Moreover such an agency might frequently use its resources in collaboration with private capital.

Such an agency would be different from the IRC in crucial respects. It would not be a single-purpose agency, concerned only with mergers. It would be responsible to government and Parliament in a more clear-cut way than the IRC ever was. It would not be subject to the limitations imposed on the IRC in respect of the holding of equity. It would carry a much heavier burden of responsibility for the results of its interventions. It could not be run on a shoestring. It might, at the outset, be even less acceptable to industry than was, at first, the IRC. But we have come a long way since the IRC. Selective intervention is now respectable. A responsible agency for the conduct of selective intervention might quite soon become not so much acceptable to industry—that was one of the faults of the IRC—but a respected source of new competition from which industry generally and the national economy would be felt to benefit.

The argument as to whether or not there should be a para-governmental agency is sometimes limited to whether or not in the judgment of one commentator or another, civil servants have the skill and experience for this type of job; whether or not one can get into the Civil Service businessmen of the required calibre; whether a government department can ever be as flexible and urgent in its approach to industrial problems as can such an agency. These are important questions. But there is also the question of whether it is not necessary or at least desirable, given the expected extension of government intervention in industry, to ensure that wherever it can be done, a proper framework of responsibility is constructed; and to ensure also that where the objectives of intervention are social or imperial rather than economic, or where, as in the case of the aluminium smelters, there are such wide political implications and such great friction within government itself to overcome, those cases should not be properly specified and explained.

Chapter 9

TOWARDS CRITERIA FOR
INDUSTRIAL POLICY

1. *Case-Work in the Public Interest*

Political parties give hostages to fortune when they claim to
be able to raise the long-term growth rate of the economy
within the lifetime of a Parliament by means evidently secret
from their political opponents. The inherent unlikelihood of
there being such secrets is illustrated not only by the con-
troversies among economists as to the sources of economic
growth, but by such simple facts as the time it takes to build
a power station, a major chemical factory or a motorway.
Even if a new government held a whole portfolio of economic
secrets, worked out no doubt on computers at party head-
quarters, it would take some years before the benefit could
be seen. In fact political parties are not original thinkers on
economic matters. They have no such secrets. They are
merely eclectic purveyors of fashionable economic wisdom.
The most that the economic wisdom of this age permits is the
unsophisticated but not inherently improbable belief that it
is more likely that the long-term growth rate will be stretched
if the economy itself is stretched by demand, than if it is
compressed by deflation. This belief is what is meant by the
assertion, popular among politicians, that a 'higher priority'
should be given to economic growth.

The danger of such claims is, first of all, disappointment
and disillusion in the electorate at large, a serious danger
because of the effect on the reputation of democratic institutions and hence on the authority of government. But there is
also the danger that a government may delay accommodating
its policies to economic reality in the belief that it can change
economic reality in short order. Thus, for example, it may be

led to delay a necessary devaluation or an equally necessary withdrawal from over-expensive commitments, whether military commitments east of Suez or technological commitments on the frontiers of knowledge; or it may exaggerate the effect of competition or incentives or of entry into Europe, or even the confidence-creating effect on industry of the return of a Conservative government, and then find itself operating a series of interventionist policies, a million miles from Selsdon Park,[1] which only a skilled political phrasemaker could significantly differentiate from those of its predecessors.

Industrial policy is too often seen in the 'growth' context. In Chapter 3 we discussed the dangers of simple insights into industrial processes which led, in one case there illustrated, to the fiction of industrial logic. It was because industrial policy was seen in the growth context that such simple insights were sought and found. Industrial policy ideally is intelligent action by government or its agents to inject the public interest into specific industrial situations. Industrial policy is casework in the public interest.

If such action is well-handled, it may have a beneficial effect on the growth rate. If it is badly handled, it may have a deleterious effect. But there is no identifiable link between these micro-economic interventions and macro-economic effects. In the Department of Economic Affairs, in the days when doubts were beginning to creep in, it was sometimes asked, mainly in jest, how many micros made a macro. It is no more than an illustrative exaggeration to say that that question was really like asking how many apples make a ton of coals. Micros and macros are two different orders and qualities of activity.

When an industrial company makes an investment it probably hopes thereby to expand its output, to expand its share of a market or at least to maintain its share of an expanding market, and to make a profit. It may think that its investment is making a small but useful contribution to national prosperity and economic growth. But it has no

[1] See *Sunday Times* editorial, 5 November 1972

guarantee even if it is a large industrial company that, when all the increments of investment made by all industrial companies are added up within the economic system, there will necessarily be a change in the rate of economic growth. All its investment may have served to do is sustain the past rate of economic growth. It may indeed not have been enough to achieve even that end.

When a government makes an investment in a firm somewhere in industry, it will hope to achieve some beneficial, and preferably identifiable, effect by that intervention. But it will have no more guarantee than does a private company that an effect identifiable in the circumstances of the firm will be equally identifiable in an enhanced growth rate. In every economy every year a milliard of separate decisions are being made which affect the working of the economy. In terms of growth rate, many of them may cancel others out. The government cannot conceivably intervene in all to make sure that they all operate in the same beneficial direction. Certainly it can intervene in some and it can influence a few of the more important. But it should concentrate its mind on the justification of the individual intervention and not try to extrapolate from it either to macro-economic effects or to principles of intervention that will have macro-economic effects.

This is not to say that if governments are prepared to make large expenditures, they may not have large effects. There have been large expenditures on aerospace and as a result we have an aerospace industry. There have been large expenditures on regional policy and this has certainly served to move some employment and to create other employment. Where expenditures are so large, they are particularly likely to have side-effects which must be assessed in practice alongside the direct purposes. This is an uncertain business and therefore even in these cases it may be impossible to identify with any certainty the effect on the growth rate of the economy as a whole.

In other words, the justification of industrial policy lies in the merit of the individual interventions from the point of view of some defensible judgment of the public interest.

Because the public interest in industrial matters is an elusive concept, it will be impossible to write other than the most general criteria for the governance of industrial policy.

The evident need for industrial interventions to be individually justified entitles a government to be sceptical of statements of the kind: 'We need large firms in Europe, and therefore we need large transnational European companies, if we are to compete with the large American multinationals.' There may be cases where this is true. The Dunlop–Pirelli merger does not appear to have been such a case, but there may be better examples. If there are, let each example be justified by the benefits expected to accrue and not from some general principle of comparable size.

If the approach is to be thus pragmatic, the simple insights on the other side of the argument must equally be avoided. One statement frequently found is: 'Industrial policy will simply slow the adaptation of the company to new competitive situations and therefore will defeat its own ends.' Undoubtedly there are such interventions, made in the name of industrial policy, which have that effect. But a long list of interventions could be specified which did not have that effect, unless it be argued that anything the state does which eases the burden of businessmen is tending to keep them in activities they would better quit. Let us try a *reductio ad absurdum*: 'If a businessman needs the benefit of government advisory services, he would do better to transfer his resources to an activity where he would not need that benefit.'

A similar pragmatism requires governments to consider the actual rather than simply the theoretical impact on their national economies of international competition. Here the example presently to be watched is Japan. If Japan places voluntary export curbs on her industries at a time of large trade surplus with the UK, that will temporarily benefit UK industry and employment. As however no one in the UK will know how long the curbs will operate, no one will be prepared to gamble money by way of investment in industries liable to be swamped. The relative competitiveness of Japanese industry is likely to continue to improve. A British govern-

TOWARDS CRITERIA FOR INDUSTRIAL POLICY 225

ment would be entitled to conclude that voluntary export curbs are not the kind of trade reciprocity that has much use for Britain.

The case where I have shown myself most prepared to move towards a principle of industrial policy has been in competition policy. This has been primarily in order to create an entry for pragmatic enquiry into more positions of actual or potential market dominance, and by means of a new presumption, to shift slightly the balance of decision by the Monopolies Commission as to the public interest particularly in merger situations. Yet competition policy is different from other interventions of industrial policy. It is directly concerned with the maintenance of choice. It therefore preserves a dimension of freedom in society. At this point in the argument, it is ends rather than means that are under focus, and to ends anyone is entitled to give his own personal, possibly eccentric, valuation.

It is right to treat very seriously warnings about political pressures on governments with money to spend in industry, whether those political pressures derive from direct electoral considerations or from a feeling that the national pride will not be sufficiently stroked except by formidable expenditures on prestige projects. Yet we have recently had striking demonstration of the fact that these dangers are not avoided by religious vows swearing disengagement from industry and marriage only to *laissez-faire*. The best that can be done is to establish a stronger framework of responsibility and more effective checks and balances. It is certainly no use bewailing intervention, because the tears will not wash away the policy. For that there are two good reasons. The first is that political pressures do represent something of which governments are right to take account. The second is that there is no rational reason for refraining from intervention in the fact that intervention is often badly handled. Governments will act because it seems sensible to act, as well as because it sometimes seems politically convenient. It is certainly right to set up a screening mechanism to protect the public. But the fact that governments sometimes get drunk does not make it practical to introduce prohibition in Whitehall.

H

There is likely to be more industrial policy in the world in future rather than less. One reason is that some governments, and this includes both the UK and the US governments, have become dissatisfied with the actual operation of the international trading system. They will want to make more certain in future that it operates to their benefit, and industrial policy will be one method they will use. Another reason is that while Europe still feels compelled to depend on the USA for military protection it is less prepared to depend on it so absolutely in the advanced technologies, and sees less need because there is less danger. It will be sensible for the poorer countries of Western Europe, such as ourselves, to oppose collective expenditures concerned with no other object than competitive pride. We can afford to delay a little before the first European is landed on the moon,

But the overriding reason why there will be more industrial policy is that national governments have responsibilities and will see industrial policies as a way of discharging them, even though there are acknowledged risks of waste.

The development of industrial policy is, however, one further expression of the ever more pervasive activities of governments. The central question, therefore, which is thrown up by industrial policy is how shall these pervasive policies be controlled to ensure that there is some public interest to which they can reasonably be claimed to respond. In other countries this question may be easier to resolve. The US Congress did once turn down the idea of an American answer to Concorde. But in this country, with a Parliament exercising less control over its government than any other Western European Parliament outside France, this is a difficult, perhaps insoluble, problem. International pressures can sometimes provide some protection, but in an age of costly collaborative projects we can as easily find ourselves drawn forward into, rather than held back from, expensive adventures. It is with this problem in mind that the three criteria in the next section have been drafted. It would be unwise to overestimate the protection they would afford. We are terribly dependent on the judgment of ministers.

2. *Three Criteria*

Bertrand Russell had three principles of scepticism which, he said, were mild yet if accepted would absolutely revolutionise human life. Probably the most controversial of his three principles was that when the experts are agreed, the opposite opinion cannot be held to be certain.[2]

Likewise there are three criteria which should determine government intervention in industry. Again they are mild and unsurprising. Even if they were accepted, they could not absolutely revolutionise government activity in this area. Yet they are implicit in what has been written here and they are worth repeating. They are as follows:

1. That action will be in the public interest.
2. That it should be defensible as being in the public interest.
3. That someone will be responsible and that his identity will be knowable.

Let us examine these criteria one by one.

(a) *That action will be in the public interest.* In Chapter 2, I said that, whereas it was possible to illustrate the view different governments have taken of the public interest, it was seldom in industrial policy possible to define it in advance of the consideration of specific issues. Nevertheless cumulative illustration does give some guide to the weighting that should be attached to the different considerations which have to be balanced against one another. This book has indicated the importance of the social factor in industrial policy. It has argued that a greater weight should be allowed to the preservation of competition than has been typical of postwar governments. It has emphasised that means are important as well as ends, if for no better reason than that ill-chosen means can defeat the ends, and that therefore a public interest determination by government must have regard to the nature of the means as well as to the desirability of the end. Amidst the uncertainties, therefore, there are guide-lines.

2 Bertrand Russell *Let the People Think* (Thinker's Library no. 84) p. 2

Yet the overall message is against over-simple views and in favour of a readiness in government to consider issues on their merits in the individual case. The role of political principle is to set a direction to society. But even knowledge of one's direction will not always help with navigation through each particular obstacle on the route.

(b) *That it should be defensible as being in the public interest.* To determine whether an action is defensible, one simple method is to require that, in appropriate cases, it be defended. It should be possible to show that there is a reasonable probability of a net positive benefit to the community.[3] The more important actions should have to be defended at the time they are initiated. Lesser actions might be subject to enquiry retrospectively where such enquiry appears to be necessary. This is where an improved Public Accounts Committee such as described in Chapter 8 would come into its own. It would select government decisions for enquiry, criticism and questioning. Decision-makers of whatever level would be asked to explain the reasons for the decisions and why it was expected that the objective would be achieved by the means proposed. The fact that this might happen, and happen soon, would concentrate the minds of decision-makers. In the major cases, where enquiry was more or less contemporary with the decision, the minister himself could appear to justify his action and not leave it to an accounting officer some years later, who may not even have advised on the decision, let alone have any responsibility for it.

There may be concern that the too-rigorous enforcement of such a criterion would bring industrial policy to a halt. But at the moment ministers are supposed to be able to defend the decisions they take in reply to questioning or debate. The proposal here would simply make the system of parliamentary control slightly more effective. It would do something to make the theory of the constitution coincide

[3] In *Subsidy Issues in International Commerce* Chapter 6 (Trade Policy Research Centre), Geoffrey Denton and Seamus O'Cleireacain suggest criteria by which the trade effect of a subsidy can be assessed. The trade effect is only one aspect of the public interest. But their suggested criteria are relevant to the assessment of the public interest.

with the practice. Moreover under our system of government, ministers who appeared before the PAC would have the comfort that their own party was in a majority upon it.

(c) *That someone will be responsible and that his identity will be knowable.* This criterion once more is entirely in accord with the theory of the constitution, if not with all its contemporary practice. Contemporary practice has been discussed in Chapter 7. Responsibility in this context does not just mean responsibility for the intervention but also for deciding what degree of control is necessary as a follow-up from the action. Control will usually be necessary to maximise the chances of the action achieving its planned effects. There will be less of a tendency to see the taking of a decision as the end of involvement. What the country requires from ministers and civil servants is not persuasive explanations as to why good decisions went wrong in application, but effective efforts to ensure that the flow of action arising from good decisions was in fact directed to, and likely to achieve, the planned objective. Of course mistakes will be made but it has never been considered—at any rate outside government— that the inevitability of mistakes is a reason for blurring responsibility.

It may seem unusual to place such emphasis on responsibility. In the Appendix will be found an important answer given by Sir Antony Part, Permanent Secretary of DTI, to the Public Accounts Committee when he was discussing certain aspects of the relationship between a government and a company that it had decided to help. It will be observed how infrequently the word 'responsibility' appears, and then only when the fear is expressed that action by the government may have the impermissible effect of transferring responsibility from the board of directors to the government. The emphasis placed in this book on the responsibility of government arises from the conviction that despite all the technical advances in the system of government, it is the judgment of individuals, officials and ministers that remains decisive. That being so, the need for the ancient discipline of responsibility is still paramount.

3. *Of Judgment*

It has always been known that a key element in the successful formulation and application of policy is judgment. There are people who have good judgment and people who have bad judgment. Recently a multiplicity of aids to judgment has been developed, to such an extent indeed that the crucial importance of judgment would be overlooked were it not still an everyday experience that despite all the techniques, decision-makers still come to different conclusions upon the evidence. Barbara Wootton has criticised the 'mystique of judgment'[4] and has written of the social scientist already deserving a place 'in the ante-chamber to certainty'.[5] Ministers and officials find themselves far too infrequently for their ease of mind resident in that particular ante-chamber. The searching eye of judgment selects a few acceptable courses of action from a multitude of possible courses which calculation may suggest. It then decides on one. How it does it, we do not know, how to train it we do not know. But it is the great factor and it cannot be replaced. It does however need to be informed.

Yet there are aids to judgment of which cost-benefit analysis is one, and it is sensible if government avails itself of them. Cost-benefit analysis, for example, may help in systematically opening up a problem. It can help to identify the elements in a problem, and even an attempt to measure immeasurable factors such as quiet, beauty and antiquity, will make the decision-maker aware that in his decision he may be in fact measuring them even though he does not do so explicitly. A minister or official, therefore, who simply sat down at his desk and proceeded without further aid or further exploration to make his judgment about complex problems would simply show poor judgment.

It has been observed that good judgment does not necessarily require high intellectual capacity. People who lack high intelligence, which to some extent may be measurable, have often thought themselves to be compensated by what they

4 Barbara Wootton *In a World I Never Made* (Allen and Unwin) pp. 216-17
5 ibid., p. 216

take to be their 'good judgment', a characteristic which is not measurable and which clever people do not always possess. Thus esteem for good judgment which all may consider they have, rather than for intellectual brilliance which admittedly had been shared unequally, is a most democratic sentiment. As Hobbes put it:

> Such is the nature of man, that however they may acknowledge many others to be more witty, or more eloquent, or more learned: yet they will hardly believe there be many so wise as themselves; for they see their own wit at hand and other men's at a distance. But this proveth rather that men are in that point equal, than unequal. For there is not ordinarily a greater sign of the equal distribution of anything, than that every man is contented with his share.[6]

It is comforting to discover that so important a property can be thought to be so equally shared, the more so as it is a property so relevant to the ministerial conduct of industrial policy.

[6] Thomas Hobbes *Leviathan* (Everyman's Library) p. 63

Appendix

Answer by Sir Antony Part, K.C.B., M.B.E., Permanent Secretary, Department of Trade and Industry, at Meeting with the Public Accounts Committee on 8 March 1972

1. I think that when a Government intervenes to help a company four problems may arise. The four problems are interconnected, but it may be helpful to spell them out separately. In order not to complicate the picture I am assuming that the help is to come direct from Government and not through an agency such as the SIB.

2. The *first* problem is that because the help comes from Government other people may think that the Government will be prepared to go on propping the company up whatever happens. The *second* is that the Government must avoid getting itself into a position that would cause a private person to fall foul of Section 332 of the Companies Act. The *third* is that if the information about the company's performance and prospects is insufficient the public investment in the company may be endangered before the Government becomes aware of the facts. The *fourth* is that if on the other hand the Government asks for too much information and intervenes with too many queries or suggestions it may erode the freedom of action of the directors to an extent that will appear to diminish their responsibility for the management of the company and give the outside world the impression that the Government's commitment to the company is greater than the Government intended.

3. I do not think there is any single or perfect answer to these questions because circumstances vary so much from case to case, but perhaps there are some useful pointers.

4. The first, I suggest, is to get a clear statement of the state of the company and its prospects at the time when the Government is contemplating putting money in. This sounds an extremely elementary thing to say, but I am not sure that history proves that it has always happened.

5. The second is the need for the Government to make clear the basis on which the help is being given, and by 'basis' in this context, I mean that if, for example, the Government estimate—no doubt on advice—that it will be some three or four years before a company can attain anything that could be described as com-

mercial viability, then the length of that bridge ought to be known about, so that everyone understands where they stand so far as the assumptions on which any aid is being given are concerned.

6. The third pointer is the need to make clear the extent of the Government's involvement, and I expect the Committee will by now have seen the written Answer which the Chief Secretary gave yesterday and which is intended to provide the normal frame of reference. What the Chief Secretary said was that those doing business with a limited liability company in which the Government has a financial interest must act on the assumption that liability for the company's debt will be determined solely in accordance with the normal rules applicable to a limited liability company under the Companies Acts, except where the Government undertakes or has undertaken a specific commitment in relation to those debts. That is the further statement which the Chairman of the Public Accounts Committee was, I think, seeking in the debate on the Committee's last report.

7. The fourth pointer—and here I am trying to take into account what has or has not happened in a number of previous cases—is that the Government should agree with the company the nature and frequency of any returns that the company is to render to the Government. That again sounds simple, but a great deal of careful thought may be needed about the key indicators that should find a place in these returns. These discussions about returns ought also to cover any points that the Government wants to check about the company's management information and accounting systems, and the way they work or are to work . . . Incidentally, all this business about returns should help to ensure that the right information comes to the attention of the Board and senior management from within the company. I have a glancing reference to that also a little later on.

8. Fifthly, these formal returns should be adequately supplemented by informal contacts between the Chairman and the Government, and the same goes of course for the Government director if there is one.

9. Sixthly, all these arrangements must not be such as to remove the prime responsibility and main focus of initiative from the Board of the company. That may sometimes be quite a difficult balance to hold, but it is very important that it should be held.

10. The Government must have the necessary expertise for monitoring the information they receive. They can and sometimes should, and sometimes do, use outside accountants and merchant

banks for this purpose; but I am sure they need to have a good continuing capability of their own. If I may interject one point here, my own experience suggests that Government should be particularly wary when information begins to show a tendency to come in late.

11. All that is easier said than done. The problems are, I believe, genuinely difficult ones and they have often defeated even distinguished accountants and merchant banks. Perhaps it is fair to remember that when companies are getting into trouble—or failing to get out of trouble—they tend to become secretive; not only the Board of companies, but people within companies tend to become secretive *vis-à-vis* the Board.

12. Finally, even if all the things that I have mentioned are done, and done successfully, the path of Ministers and civil servants is not going to be made smooth. The potential options open to them will often be dramatic, and damaging either to a company or the Exchequer. What one can hope is that if the pointers that I have described are followed the frame in which Government help is set will be clearer, the extent of the Government's commitment will be more explicit, and the early warning systems better than they have sometimes been in the past.

Third Report of the Public Accounts Committee 1971-72 (Q.1548)

Index

238 POLITICAL RESPONSIBILITY AND INDUSTRY